D0407959

Every QUILT Tells a Story

A Quilter's Stash of Wit and Wisdom

Helen Kelley

Voyageur Press

A TOWN SQUARE BOOK

Text copyright © 2003 by Helen Kelley

All rights reserved. No part of this work may be reproduced or used in any form by any means—graphic, electronic, or mechanical, including photocopying, recording, taping, or any information storage and retrieval system—without written permission of the publisher.

Edited by Margret Aldrich
Designed by Maria Friedrich
Printed in China

03   04   05   06   07   5   4   3   2   1

Library of Congress Cataloging-in-Publication Data

Kelley, Helen, 1927–
  Every quilt tells a story : a quilter's stash of wit and wisdom / Helen Kelley.
      p. cm.
"A Town Square book."
  ISBN 0-89658-623-5 (hardback)
  1. Quilting—United States—Miscellanea. 2. Patchwork—United States—Miscellanea. 3. Quilts—United States—Miscellanea. I. Title.
  TT835 .K45 2003
  746.46—dc21

                              2002012140

Published by Voyageur Press, Inc.
123 North Second Street, P.O. Box 338, Stillwater, MN 55082 U.S.A.
651-430-2210, fax 651-430-2211
books@voyageurpress.com
www.voyageurpress.com

Educators, fundraisers, premium and gift buyers, publicists, and marketing managers: Looking for creative products and new sales ideas? Voyageur Press books are available at special discounts when purchased in quantities, and special editions can be created to your specifications. For details contact the marketing department at 800-888-9653.

Dedication

To Bonnie Leman and Mary Leman Austin.

⊠ ⊠ ⊠

CONTENTS

⊠ ⊠ ⊠

PREFACE

I am a quiltmaker, purely and simply put. There is no need to explain that to another quilter. To a non-quiltmaker, however, the compulsion to "cut fabric into little pieces and sew them back together again" (as the non-quilt world puts it) is a puzzlement. The astonishing satisfaction that comes from quilting is beyond explanation.

Be that as it may, the fact is that I spend my days surrounded by loose threads, quilt-square clippings, and stacks of folded fabric. Long sinuous fibers trim my workroom rug and cling to my clothing. Scraps of appliquéd pieces and colorful quilt blocks lie like confetti around me. The coveted quilter's stash surrounds me in growing towers of calico and muslin.

I am a hand-quilter and because of that, I spend long hours at the quilt frame. Non-quilters marvel at my persistence and my concentration. I will confess that hand-quilting, for me, gives me the time and opportunity to mull over the State of the World, and the State of Helen. Consequently, if I am able to break my mind away from the steady rhythm of the rising and falling of my needle, I can jot down the thoughts that drift through my mind and try to capture a few of those mental threads and the stories that go with them, putting them down on paper to share with my quilting friends.

I did not start out to be a quiltmaker. Long ago and far away, I thought that I was going to be an actress. I actually studied for the stage, and though I do not know now if I would ever have been a successful Ophelia or Eliza, acting taught me some really important quiltmaking skills. For one thing, I learned endurance. Acting is very hard work with long hours of rehearsal, daily discipline, and total commitment. Acting also taught me to look at the world around me and to discover it and to love it and to relive it. There are lots of things we all do in our lives that teach these precious lessons, but for me, it was the acting experience that helped me learn to focus.

In 1946, during the aftermath of World War II, I became engaged to marry a Marine and I began my first quilt. I spent two years making my wedding quilt, and because I knew no other quilters, my quiltmaking processes were basically invented. It was sheer happenstance that I was actually able to produce that quilt.

This is how I went about it. I studied a quilt that had belonged to my mother, and using a long-forgotten kit that she had stored in the bottom of a drawer for forty-five years, I appliquéd large quilt squares of purple daisies and green leaves. I trimmed the edges of the appliqué with tiny buttonhole stitches and manipulated the entire assemblage of stitched flowers and alternate Nile green blocks into a double-bed-sized quilt. How I managed that out-of-control conglomeration is still a mystery. The top, cotton batt, and sheet were layered and stitched together in long, parallel, diagonal lines. I thought it was beautiful. These many years later, the sentiment is still beautiful. I realize, now, that aesthetically, it falls somewhat short.

Over the succeeding years, and through the raising of five children, my quiltmaking improved, but my occasional flight into textile fancies was actually a survival technique. In the midst of a rambunctious, creative family, quilting held my mind together and kept my sanity intact.

Through the early 1970s, my life resembled the ruffled and flouncy world of TV's *The Donna Reed Show*. My house was clean. The meals that I made daily and on time were nutritious and attractive. Wherever we went as a family, all seven of us were outfitted in identical clothes—matching dresses and shirts created with my trusty Featherweight sewing machine. Early in that decade, my oldest daughter decided to get married. A wedding quilt seemed appropriate, and I challenged my friends and assorted relatives to make squares for that quilt.

It was an ambitious undertaking. Those neophytes had no clue as to how to go about the project, but I cajoled and encouraged them to send me counted thread and needle-pointed and painted pictures which I cut to size and pieced into a double-bed-sized quilt. I sandwiched the layers together and gave a quilting party to initiate my friends into the mysteries of stitching their blocks into a soft, sweet wedding blessing. They came, excited to be part of the celebration, and took their first, halting quilting stitches. The local newspaper thought all of this activity was very quaint and came out and took pictures. When the article about the quilt appeared in the paper, my phone began to ring and I found three more quilters. In fact, I found quilters four and five. When we gathered together, we formed a quilters' support group.

For that first meeting, we went to lunch. As you well know, next to quilts, a quiltmaker's favorite thing is food. We were hungry women who had longed to talk to someone about color and fabric and patterns. Over a crispy salad and a sinful dessert, we became immediate friends. These women taught mostly in adult education programs, and we shared our quilting secrets, our teaching hints, and methods of coping with underheated winter classrooms and deserted nighttime parking lots. We talked about where we could find the few yards of cotton fabric available (remember that this was during the early 1970s when most people were having love affairs with double knits and polyesters). We discussed how to load the long poles of quilt frames into our cars and the advantages of giant quilting hoops. We had come to our luncheon rather shyly, but we left as fast friends.

Most of those women that day were self-taught. Only a couple had learned to quilt "at their grandmother's knee." All of them shared an esteem and respect for history and an appreciation for the inheritance that early quilters have left us.

It was a strange time. Quilting had almost disappeared in the United States. In the 1940s, factory-made bedding had become readily available and affordable. During World War II,

- - - -

many women worked long hours at one, and sometimes two, jobs. They had little time or need for quilts, and the craft of quilting drifted into obscurity. After the war, we plunged into the excitement of TV and an eclectic array of electrical appliances and shiny cars. If quilting was mentioned in magazines, it was as a charming, curious skill from once-upon-a-time.

Those of us who were quilters and met that day around the luncheon table had somehow heard a siren's song. I think, somewhere in that time, each of us had been bewitched by the creative possibilities of quilting, and all of us had an inherited love for fabric.

With the coming of the Bicentennial celebration of 1976, magazines picked up on our colonial heritage and printed full-color articles on quilts. I remember standing in line at the grocery store, leafing through the magazines arrayed there, looking for pictures—any pictures of quilted pillows and potholders. Then, the contests began. They offered generous prizes for "Bicentennial quilts." New quilt shops with exciting classes began to sprout along the streets among the neighborhood stores. Suddenly, people began to discover the joys of creating something, not because it was needed, but because it was enormously satisfying to make something beautiful with their own hands.

Now, in the quiet after the storm of excitement that had swirled around my daughter's wedding quilt, there was time to sit back and survey my lifestyle. I had, for all the years of my married life, made slipcovers, curtains, party dresses, coats, and costumes. I had just finished several bridesmaid's dresses and a wedding dress with a long, pearled train. I was weary from fitting and tweaking, tucking, pleating, and ruffling. Then and there, I decided that instead of dressmaking, I would devote myself to making quilts, which do, after all, lie flat and have square corners.

By the end of the 1970s, I had found seventeen other quilting friends, and we did what quilters do—we organized formally. A tax-accountant volunteered to be treasurer and a librarian volunteered to be secretary. Being president seemed to require no previous experience of any kind whatsoever, and I found that I was exceptionally well-qualified.

The new quilt guild produced a newsletter, of course, and it seemed reasonable to assume that, as president, I would write some kind of article that would fill up the space between the listing of officers and the calendar for the coming month. Those ramblings were the seeds of my first "Loose Threads" articles. I began to write for *Quilter's Newsletter Magazine* in the early 1980s.

My articles are paper conversations. They are spun out in my workroom, amidst my daily life. I come and go here, sometimes stop to prepare meager meals, and generally live in the midst of snippings and threads. I will quite honestly admit, however, that making meals, cleaning house, doing laundry, and running errands have a very low priority in my life. My regular readers in *Quilter's Newsletter Magazine* know that I am blessed with an understanding, tolerant, and supportive husband named Bill. I may sigh about him. I may raise my eyebrows about him and murmur laments about him, but, truth be told, he holds my life together. Bill is a methodical engineer, and I am an absent-minded dreamer. I am grateful for him and his leveling influence. He is a good man.

I am also blessed, or cursed, with a talent for getting myself into fixes. It happens that I am an impulsive sort of person, and I hurl myself into my work with abandon. Sometimes—usually—I find myself in a mess. When I work late into the night, I snip holes in places where there are not supposed to be holes. I trip over iron cords. I spill coffee. I tip pins onto the floor. I break sewing machine needles. Actually, among quilters this is more the rule than the exception, and like other quilters, I rise from my disasters like a phoenix rising from the flames. I write about my frailties, and others write to me about theirs. There is a universality in quilts and the threads that hold them together—those wonderful, comforting, touchy-feely threads that are on our worktables and our clothing and in our minds. Because of this bond, we can talk to each other, machine-quilters and hand-quilters, clippers and cutters, dippers and dyers, and, yes, non-quilting friends, spouses, and sometimes even strangers.

People who deal with quilts—those who stitch them, collect them, and admire them—have what I call a "Q-chromosome." Genetically speaking, that Q-chromosome is made up of those things we all have in common. Q-chromosome people tend to save fabric in big heaps and sketch geometric designs on available newspapers, scratch pads, and the backs of store receipts. Q-people frequently talk to themselves while solving heavy problems that have to do with color and visual value. When Q-people go on vacation, they will most probably each carry along a sewing machine that has the approximate weight of an anvil.

Q-people create lots of loose threads, stories, and memories. Q-people like each other, and I like them, and that is what I write about.

When my children grew up, they moved out of the house, but not out of my mind. They still come back now and then. They call me on the phone. They offer me advice and give me orders, to which I rarely pay any attention. They bring their children and grandchildren for me to adore; I make them all quilts. These many years later, with the help of a microwave oven and an occasional swish of a spongy floor mop to do the chores, I am free to spend my time in the way that makes me most happy—with my quilts.

This has become a way of life. My house is marginally acceptable, and Bill is generous and forbearing, bless him; he encourages me. I stitch. I smile. I am happy, and I produce lots of loose threads and stories of my own.

Chapter 1

THREADS OF WISDOM

Kelley's Laws for Quilters

FIRST LAW

The woman in the line ahead of you at the store will buy the last half yard of the fabric you wanted.

SECOND LAW

If you use up your favorite fabric today, it will be exactly what you will need to finish tomorrow's project.

THIRD LAW

When ironing any unknown fabric with a hot iron, you will discover that it has a polyester content.

FOURTH LAW

The quilt book you put in a safe place for quick reference will be lost forever.

FIFTH LAW

When a bad seam is sewn a second time, it will always be worse than the first.

SIXTH LAW

When sewing one more seam before going to bed, you will catch your elbow in the pin dish.

SEVENTH LAW
The burr on your scissors blade will fall exactly at the place where precision is most important.

EIGHTH LAW
A 12" block will always measure 12½" on one side and 11¾" on the opposite side.

NINTH LAW
The distance a spool of thread will roll under the quilting frame is equal to the length of your arm plus one inch.

TENTH LAW
When you have pricked your finger with a quilting needle, you will always assume that the prick is not deep enough to bleed on your white fabric.

ELEVENTH LAW
A lost quilting needle is a misery in the foot.

TWELFTH LAW
The joy of each day is directly proportionate to the hours spent in quilting.

My Mama Done Tol' Me

It was 1:30 A.M. before I finally got to bed. I've been working on a quilt. Every day has been a new adventure, and the lovely thing about this quilt is that it has been so satisfying. Everything I have done has been right. The design fell into place as if it had been planned eons before the world began and was always meant to be this way. When I went out to buy the fabric, I couldn't find the right red. I bought a second choice and when I got it home, it was perfect—far better than what I had been hoping for. It was as if somebody had said, "No, no, no. Not this one. THAT red." Even though the colors came from different stores, they flowed through gradations of gold and turquoise as smoothly as if I had dyed them. The piecing I had designed looked complicated, but on closer examination, I discovered a logical progression. Each block went together smoothly, points sharp and precise.

Then came last night.

Nothing I did was right. I ripped seams three, four, and even five times. The fabric was limp. I tried to restitch over the old needle holes. The edges got hairier and hairier. My precious old sewing machine chunked along with funny noises and routinely snagged and made great knots underneath the piecing. I made mental notes to oil the machine, to try a new needle. Did this needle have a burr on it? Was the eye shredding the thread? Or was the thread itself causing the trouble?

It was wiry and it fluffed up and refused to go through the needle's eye every time it snapped. Even my wire threader bent into an odd, twisty shape and refused to poke through the eye.

The corners of my fabric kept catching in the steam vents of my iron and shriveling up. I took to licking them to dampen the corners before pressing them flat because dabbing water on them became an interminable, repetitive process.

Piecing always gives me pleasure. That's why I do it. I love to piece; I love to watch all those scraps multiply into dazzling whole blocks. Why, then, did I persist last night until 1:30 A.M., struggling with things that obviously had a mind of their own?

Late at night was not an intelligent time to be working. I was tired, I was tense, and, oh boy, was I determined! I knew that I was going to make the whole thing work if it killed me. Looking at those precious pieced blocks this morning, I see that they are fine. They are flat and precise. I wonder if I had had the strength of character to put them aside when it was obvious that things were not working right, if I could have done them later in a fraction of the time and with real pleasure. What makes me persist?

As a child, all those years ago, I remember hearing the old axiom, "If at first you don't succeed, try, try again." I can hear my mother chanting it to me; I can see my schoolteachers writing it on the blackboard. I probably even jumped rope to the beat of that chant. I clearly recall hopping down the stairs: "IF at FIRST you DON'T sucCEED, TRY, and TRY aGAIN."

People call this character trait "sticktuitivity." It is supposed to be a good attribute. I wonder! In comparing notes on working habits with other quilters, I have frequently wondered if the good Germanic element in my background is the compelling force that makes me say, "I will do this. I will do it right, even if I have to stay up all night." The process nearly undoes me.

I tell my friends, if your piecing is not working for you, for goodness sake, go next door for a cup of coffee or to the quilt shop to buy some fabric or just go to bed! I myself do not have the strength of character to do this.

Maybe I need to erase that old "If at first" record that plays hauntingly in my head. Maybe I need to make a new one. Let's see, what should it say? I know! From this moment on when it becomes obvious that my thread and I are getting all tied up in knots, I shall recite: "Put it down and do it later; better work and joy that's greater!"

All together now. PUT it DOWN and DO it LATer; BETter WORK and JOY that's GREATer. Once again. PUT it DOWN and DO it LATer; BETter WORK and JOY. . . .

Lesson Learned from a Munchkin

It was obvious when I stood in front of my closet this morning that there was nothing to wear. Everything that hung in its dark recesses was either ten years old or thirty pounds heavier. Any of my skirts or sweaters or dresses that I slipped myself into would make me look like Auntie Em. There comes a time when we all face the same crisis in our lives. We must either be dowdy or go out and spend a lot of money. I had been dowdy long enough.

When I pushed my way through the door of the department store, I found myself in a dream come true. The inside of the store was Peach City! Every mannequin was draped in peach gauze; every hanger was hung with peach jersey; every aisle was flooded with peach. You know that I am a peach lover. Ordinarily, when I go into a dress department my eye skims the clothing racks and, if there is nothing peachy, I leave with my pocketbook intact. Today was a day beyond my wildest fantasies.

In the coordinates department I slipped a peach-colored blazer off the rack. The label read, "Size 8." Surely it must have been incorrectly sized. The huge shoulders of the blazer swept out like cherub's wings. The lapels dropped straight across my chest without a hint of my body inside. The jacket buttoned somewhere below my waist. I was an absurdity! I looked like a child in her mommy's dress! I was Apple Annie and Secondhand Rose rolled into one!

I searched the racks of these contemporary garments that were all large, square, and long. My body was so far out of date that nothing, not anything in that plethora of clothing, was suitable. I had visions of myself at the next quilt symposium. I would be tacky, tacky, tacky.

A clerk appeared beside me. I asked her, "Please, do you know anything about little old ladies?"

"Certainly," she said. "My mother is one."

"Then," said I, "for goodness sake, help me."

We worked for two whole hours. In the end, we found two outfits that did not make me look like a scrap-bag lady. They were terribly expensive, but they made me look civilized. One of the handicaps of getting older is that you can remember how life used to be. Clothing used to fit. It used to cost less. I left the store in shock.

Tonight was to be the quilt-guild meeting. Young, lovely quilters would be there, looking smashing in the latest styles. Those women can wear jackets that box at the sides and button far below the belt. They are adorable in them. I dressed carefully for the meeting. My average prep time is approximately fifteen minutes. I began preening a good hour before I was to leave. I pulled my soft, downy, golden angora sweater over my head. I stepped into my skirt. It swirled around my ankles. The peach and aqua and gold plaid was bold, jaunty, adventuresome. I fastened my silk (REAL silk) scarf around my shoulders and tacked it in place with an antique pearl pin. I was gorgeous—poor, but gorgeous.

My quilted tote went into the front seat of the car. In went my purse with my membership card. Then, my boots, my gloves, my scarf, and I was off for the meeting.

The program was, as usual, great. It was a slide lecture of truly magnificent old quilts. I sat through it, posing demurely in my new outfit. Show-and-tell began. The ladies paraded across the stage in their quilted clothing. They displayed full-sized quilts and wall hangings. Directly in front of me sat a young mother with an adorable baby. He peered over her shoulder at me. He was quite the most enchanting child I had ever seen. His hair was red, his eyes bright, and his little mouth was a precious cupid's bow. In an instant I forgot that I was a glamour girl sitting there in my elegant outfit, scarf tossed casually over the shoulder, skirt draping gracefully across my knees.

"Please," I said, "may I hold him?"

His mother handed him back and we instantly fell in love. I cooed at him; I tickled him. The quilters were parading across the stage with wonderful new creations.

I bounced the baby on my knee and recited an old Norwegian nursery rhyme. "Ride, Ride, Ranke," I chanted. He gurgled uproariously and kissed me on my nose. The aides were holding up a magnificent Compass Points wall hanging, colors shaded expertly, points crisp. I flung the child into the air, then poised him on my lap, letting him brace his little legs. He chortled gleefully. "Coochie Coo!" I said. At that moment he whoopsed, laughing all the while as he decorated my beautiful gold and aqua and peach skirt that cost more than anything I had ever before bought in my whole life.

The parade on stage was over. Everyone adjourned for coffee. The quilters gathered around the refreshment table. They laughed and talked. The baby's mother bundled him into his little bunting and trundled him away. And there was I (pride goeth before a fall), sponging myself in the kitchen.

I suppose that this is the story of my life. I was never meant to be elegant or beautiful. I was meant to be me: maybe not dowdy, but certainly mature, grandmotherly, wholesome.

In all of this embarrassment, I was aware, nevertheless, that I also have some of the qualities that make me a good quiltmaker. I am experienced; certainly I am sensitive; and most especially, I know how to choose, use, and *clean* fabric!

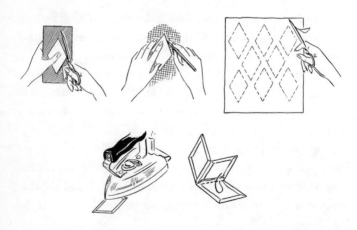

Golden Guilt

Once, a long time ago, I took a course in psychology. Most of what I studied has long been forgotten, but one thing that has remained with me all these years since was the premise that we are born without guilt. Guilt is taught to us by our parents and by society. Be that as it may, guilt is a powerful motivator. My husband, Bill, says that I am The Supreme Guilty Person, and early in life all of my daughters learned how effective it is to "lay a guilt trip" on me. I often baked twelve dozen cookies in an effort to apologize for being late for a school program or drove through rain, sleet, hail, and snow to make up for some thoughtless omission.

If guilt is a curse or a virtue that is learned, it is interesting to speculate about who taught us our compulsive behaviors. A young quilter who lives alone told me that she makes her bed once a week. I make mine every day, early in the morning, in fact, sometimes when I get out of it. My mother always did. For me, there is something sinful about an unmade bed, though I know actually that this is not true, and certainly my daughters never subscribed to that unmade-bed/sin belief.

It is interesting to note which guilts are so strong that they are driving forces and which ones simply annoy. Making my bed is a compulsion. A dirty bathroom sink simply annoys me even though that is another of the things my mother had strong feelings about. However, I will admit to dashing to my bathroom with a can of cleanser in my hand if I know that a guest is going to wash her hands.

There are guilts that require me to have supper at six on the dot because that is the way life ought to be, but for some reason, dust in my house doesn't ruffle my feathers a bit (though I will admit to apologizing compulsively about it to visitors).

Then there is the matter of my quilts. It's obvious that if we are going to make quilts that we will hang on our walls or put into quilt shows for all the world to see, we want them to be perfect. We would like everyone to know that we do nice work. If we have a quilt in the frame and the sun is golden or even if the day is dark and gloomy but we want a golden feeling in our hearts, then it is joyful to do fine quilting. There is no guilt here and we work hard, picking out bad stitches, poking in knots, marking straight, even lines, and then scrubbing out the marks after they have been quilted. This golden, guiltless joy is why we quilt loops and feathers and swirls into our quilts in empty places, why we quilt double lines beside our geometrics that bring up the riot of shapes rather than just single lines that would be quite sufficient for holding the layers together.

It is interesting to note, however, how those of us who are ordinarily guilt-laden can invent real stress in some guiltless situations. Some quilters can cheerfully coexist with astonishing numbers of unfinished projects piled in their work-rooms and feel absolutely no guilt. Then there are those of us who struggle under the virtuous burden of needing to finish things. It's as though we achieve another star in our crowns for each completed project.

Right now I have been sitting for hours at my sewing machine trying to machine quilt five hefty, little quilts. I have made one for each of my grandchildren, and I thought it would be great to have one for myself, too, to snuggle under in the evenings. I pieced the tops. They are great. I loved every moment of the cutting and stitching. Then, I stuffed a comforter batt inside each and stitched up the ends. With the whole lot basted, I topstitched around the edges.

My problem is this: In spite of the thick comforter batts, I somehow feel obligated to quilt these quilts. I am a quilter! These are too thick to get a hand-quilting needle through them, so obviously I must do them on the machine. In preparation for this quilting experiment, I went out and got myself a walking foot for my machine. I love it, so I won't place the blame on it for what has happened. In fact, that dandy new attachment may well be the only thing that is saving my sanity.

Basting pins bristled in my quilt when I sat myself down at my sewing machine, dropped the presser foot onto my work, and tromped on my machine pedal. The machine roared down the first penciled line, and it was wonderful. I began to wonder why I had never machine-quilted anything before. I rolled up the quilt and pulled the light closer and started down another line of pins. Whoopee! Look at me go! I stitched down a third side and a fourth.

I slid the quilt out from under the presser foot and picked up my scissors to trim off thread ends. I turned the quilt over. There were tucks, folds, and little pleats here and there in the stitching. My little seam ripper went to work. I snipped, I pulled, I went back to the machine and put the quilt in bottom-up! The new seams went in quickly. They looked fine on the back. The stitches on the top side, however, had not followed the seam lines. They had crisscrossed the seams and they looked shabby. More seam ripping!

A third line of stitch-ripping, and the fabric began to look weary. There were little ends of thread where I had added more stitching lines. Instead of being simply gorgeous, the whole effect was simply tacky.

I am looking at my quilts, and I am wrestling with myself. I ask myself, "What difference does it make? When I am done with my own little quilt, good or bad, it will be soft and warm. The pieced top is bright and precise. So what's the big deal? Why do I feel so miserable if it isn't perfectly quilted? What is this driving force that makes me want even this humble little thing to be lovely? Why do I feel guilty?"

Now, you see, all that guilt comes into play. I know that I cannot live with these quilts if they don't look great. I must do my best work! I will, after all, keep my own little quilt in my living room, and I will curl up in it and nightly look at those stitches.

To answer that "why guilt?" question, I think that the compulsion to make things beautiful, out of whatever guilt it is born, is a Golden Guilt. Anything that produces bits of loveliness in our lives has got to be 24 carat.

True, also, is that anything that produces headache and general irritation is Fool's Gold. Maybe those of us who are Supreme Guilters have got to learn what drives us and what's important and especially what's not really important. I think I'll relax a bit. I'll get out my yarn and tie the rest of these little quilts. I'll make comforters. I'll use the extra time and emotion and energy I save to make another quilt—something dazzling, something guiltless, something solid gold.

That's the Way the Cookie Crumbles

If my face is my fortune, I'm in big trouble. It's not a bad face—a few freckles here and there. I have a medium nose, blue eyes. It's very average, not at all what you would call "a million dollar face."

I have been fascinated with the whimsy of fortunes since I was a child. My mother used to wrap tiny symbols in waxed paper and hide them between the layers of my birthday cakes. If I got a small car, it meant that I was going on a motor trip; a boat would mean an ocean crossing; a penny foretold money; and a button was the symbol that I would be an "old maid."

We had poppers at those birthday parties, too. Do you remember poppers? They were tubes of cardboard covered with crepe-paper fringe. A tab of cardboard was buried in the paper ruffle at the end of the popper, and if you pulled the tab there would be a bang. Inside you found a paper hat, a favor, and a fortune. Mine was always a good one.

I remember Sunday evenings when I grew older and went away to school. My roommate was a beautiful, dark, mysterious Czech girl. She taught me to read fortunes in the cards. We would sit cross-legged on our beds and eat sweet apricot cookies and deal out the cards for our friends.

She was very serious about the fortunes she read. If she laid down a queen of spades, she would snap her deck of cards shut and refuse to tell you what she saw in the future. I, on the other hand, had great fun dealing and speculating. Heaven help anyone who ever took my fortune-telling seriously.

Now, when I am older but no wiser, every Sunday I check the horoscopes in the newspaper. Since my husband and I are both Tauruses, though as different as night and day, I take the good half of the fortune and let him deal with any dire warnings.

Last week, my daughter Connie came home from San Francisco, and for a present she brought us a giant bag of fortune cookies. They have wonderful fortunes inside. We can get fortune cookies in our neighborhood, but they aren't worth the effort to break them open. Last week, I got a fortune that read, "You are an honorable person." My husband's said, "Beauty is in the soul." Now, what kind of fortunes are those? A fortune should be exciting, perhaps romantic. It should tickle your imagination, promise you wonderful things. A fortune should always be good, but if it isn't, it should be dramatic. No blah fortunes for me!

Even though we are quilters, sometimes our lives need a rosy glow cast about us. After sitting much of the day over a quilt frame, we may have a feeling of contentment, but perhaps a bit of exciting speculation would add a touch of spice to our lives. When we get together to quilt with our friends, too, wouldn't it be fun to add a little intrigue to the party?

I have a wonderful idea: What about crumbling some cookies? Let's make up some great predictions and type them out and tuck them into our desserts. If you aren't a gourmet-type cook, you could slide off the top layer of a store-bought sandwich cookie and slip in the fortune.

What would these fortunes say? They could be as lavish as our minds can conjure. After all, these fortunes should fulfill our wildest dreams. We can promise our quilters the stars. For starters, how about these:

. . . You will meet a tall, dark, handsome fabric salesman.

. . . You are going on a voyage to a quilting conference.

. . . Your stitches always will be small and even.

. . . You will inherit a fabric stash.

. . . Stop searching for happiness—the fabric you need is in your sewing room.

. . . There's a blue ribbon in your future.

. . . You are going to go places—like to the quilt shop.

. . . Life is comforting. May you sleep under many quilts.

. . . If you live life on the square, you must learn to sew triangles.

And finally, . . . All good things come to those who quilt.

Recycle

A big trash bag is always tucked under my kitchen shelf. It is stuffed with all sorts of small, filmy, plastic things, grocery sacks, newspaper wrappings, bread bags, and frozen food wraps. There's a container in the back hall for tin cans and one there for plastic yogurt cups and milk bottles. Discarded glass items go into separate cardboard boxes at the foot of the basement stairs. Every other Friday, the recycle truck drives down our alley and collects our bundles of paper bags and newspapers that I have put out into the special green bin at the curb. Around it, like little satellites, are packages of glass and tin and plastic. We believe that recycling is important.

From our kitchen, our left-over orange peels and egg shells go out to be composted. A man on television shows how he makes pressed board out of recycled newspapers, and I've read about companies that make flower pots out of discarded diapers. All of this comforts us to know that some of our trash is being used again and again. I think that the urge to recycle is genetic for a quilter.

We have an amazing choice of brand new fabrics to make our quilts. The quilt stores around my home have shelves lined with hundreds and hundreds of bolts of materials. They come in all colors and an astonishing variety of patterns. I am a regular customer at these stores. I am grateful that I have these beautiful new fabrics available. We are rich with them, and it is the best kind of wealth.

Yesterday, I got a box in the mail from a friend. She comes from a lengthy line of quilters. The box was packed with fabric, pieces that she said she had collected for a long time. In that box, among the pieces of material, I found quilt pieces that had been cut and never used. There were three old shirts, part of a skirt, and the left-over armhole pieces from the makings of a dress. Some of those fabrics are one hundred years old, saved by her quilter mother or grandmother to be used, sometime, in a quilt. Those women were recyclers in the truest sense of the word.

Once, several years ago, I stored away a supply of old fabrics. Another friend was cleaning her closets, and she gave them to me. I put those fabrics into a special box, and labeled it, "Restoration." This fabric that has just come should go into that bin, to be used to repair tattered, old quilts.

I have been making a quilt block for our new guild president. Because his name is David, I thought it would be great fun to make him a wonderful old pattern of David and Goliath. Stripey fabric would be perfect for the tents, the giant, and the small boy. Last night, as I was looking for a striped piece of fabric, I happened to glance down at my new box of old fabrics. A piece of striped shirting fabric winked out at me. It called to me. Until that moment, somehow, that old fabric had seemed like a trust, to be saved because it is perfect for rescuing old quilts. It was also perfect for a tent. I used it. It was a strange experience, my using old fabric for the first time in this way.

Ordinarily, when I make a quilt, I go out and buy the fabric especially for it. I could make a hundred quilts with all of the fabric that I have stashed away, but somehow, I find it intriguing to go out and search through the bolts of material in the fabric store for exactly the right color and print. Maybe I will set myself a challenge—to make a quilt out of what I already have here, just like so many of the quilters in the past. I could recycle the bits and pieces piled in my workroom, my scraps. I could hunt through the ancient clothing that I have hung in the back of my closet, saved in case the fashions might come back in style, and I could wear them again. Why not use the beloved material in those dresses?

The shelves in the quilt stores are full of reproduction fabrics, Victorian fabrics, Depression fabrics. I don't need reproductions. I've got the real things. There is a certain mystique about quilts made with old fabrics. They talk to us of people and places and times past. They speak to us. They remind us.

On my refrigerator, there is a long list of items to be salvaged for recycling, dead batteries, lawn rakings, egg cartons, and telephone books. It is strange that it has never occurred to me before that recycling my fabric may be the biggest and best challenge of all.

_ _ _ _

Feathering My Nest

When each of us—my brother, my sister, and I—was born, our doting aunt opened a bank account for us and regularly, on birthdays and holidays, she sent us checks. We were never allowed to spend them. Instead, we went to the bank dutifully to deposit them into our accounts. We thought they were truly boring gifts.

Once when our aunt came to visit, she brought us shiny Uncle Sam banks that were shaped like black cash registers scrolled with gold lettering. Ever after, whenever she visited, she brought us each shiny quarters, and then she stood by to see us put the coins into the slots of our big black banks, pull down the levers, and watch the amounts add up in the little register windows on the front. When the quarters totaled $10, the little door in the base would open, and we were then escorted to the bank to deposit this money, too, into our accounts. All of our friends got ice cream cones and trips to the amusement parks to ride the roller coasters from their aunts.

By my twentieth birthday, my bank balance had reached a healthy figure, and being old enough by then to manage my own bank book, I withdrew my money and took it to a local shop where I purchased my first sewing machine. That machine was my beloved Singer Featherweight. I took my sewing machine away to school with me. On long evenings away from home, I sewed birthday gifts for my family.

When I was married, I decorated our first apartment. I set my machine on our new orange-crate furniture and sewed ruffly curtains for our windows. Later, after the birth of our first child, I discovered that I could make a pair of small coveralls, size one, from a printed feed sack. When the baby slept, I listened to the radio, and my Featherweight hummed cheerfully, turning out infant clothing made of pink and purple ducky and Henny-Penny chicken-feed sacking. My husband, Bill, was recalled to the Marine Corps during the Korean War. I packed up our belongings and went along with him. Back then, there was no such thing as a rental trailer to help with moving, and so we had our own utility trailer built. Packed in that big, green wooden box on wheels were our important things—the crib, the high chair, our clothing, a dish drainer, and of course, my Featherweight sewing machine in its plain black carrying case. I spent long days in military housing, tending babies, sewing little clothes, making gifts, and dabbling a bit with quilting.

When our term of duty was over, we went home. In the following years, as we raised our family, my little Featherweight was in perpetual motion. In all that time, because it was such a simple machine, I never had to have my mechanical friend repaired. It needed only oiling, cleaning, and a basic knowledge of how to keep it operating. It was light. I could pick it up with one hand and set it out on my ironing board, or a dresser, or a coffee table, anywhere, to sew. Through the years, it stitched coats, Easter outfits, and prom dresses. I dabbled, too, a bit more in quilts.

By this time, the face plate was getting scratchy and the gilt trim was fading. I noticed when I sewed in my stocking

– – – –

feet, humming along the seams so fast that you couldn't see the thread take-up arm flying up and down, that the foot pedal began to get hot. I made a trip to the sewing machine store for its first checkup. My machine was away for a week. The strain of separation was almost more than I could bear.

In 1963, I succumbed to the latest rage and bought one of those new machines that not only sewed straight seams, but had a needle that flew back and forth sideways and zigzagged the edges of my work. The new machine was a monstrous piece of equipment compared to my sturdy little Feather-weight, but it allowed me to finish clothing "professionally." I used that zigzag machine for twenty-five years. It was cumbersome and cranky and temperamental.

Whenever I wanted to do "perfect piecing," however, or if I wanted to take my quilting equipment away on a trip, I dug in the back of the closet where I had interred my Feather-weight, and I unearthed it. It still hummed cheerfully and sewed perfect, straight little stitches. It did not zigzag nor did it do embroidery, buttonholing, or blind hemming like the newest machines that were being extolled by the media in the 1980s. Every TV ad and magazine spread that touted these fancy machines enticed me. As a normal American woman, I wanted to have all the good things in life, which included a sewing machine that could do everything except cook dinner.

- - - -

Today, I have an up-to-date, modern sewing machine sitting on my workroom table that does so many things that I have to read the manual every time I use it. Yet, I still fall back on my little Featherweight from time to time. It's the machine that goes to workshops with me. It's the one I use when I want to make flawless Seminole piecing. When I am sewing on my new machine and I find that I am struggling hopelessly with my patchwork points and intersections, I get out my old Featherweight, and the little pieces seem to fall perfectly into place.

Like all of us, my little black and gold machine is aging. It's a bit noisier than it used to be. I don't remember hearing the thunka-thunka-thunka sound that it makes now as the needle bobs up and down. I hope it's just because I notice it more in comparison to my fancy machine, which is so quiet. I would like to believe that my Featherweight will last forever. Its sturdy body and precision parts seem invincible.

All those years ago, when I was putting those birthday quarters into my Uncle Sam bank, I was too young, too nearsighted to know what my wise aunt was giving to me. I thought that my friends who got shiny presents and trips to the movies from their aunts were the lucky people. I could not in my wildest dreams have known that the gift I was receiving then was the nest egg that would hatch into a lifetime treasure, my invincible Featherweight sewing machine.

– – – –

Abracadabra

I have just finished making another roll-on-the-floor quilt for a grandchild. I call them "roll-on-the-floor" quilts because that is how they are meant to be used. The children can drag them across rooms, curl up in them in front of the TV, take them for school nap time, or snuggle in them on a car trip. They can spill their cereal on them, put sticky lollipops on them, handle them with dirty fingers, and when ill, lose their lunches on them. These quilts are bright, take minimal work, are thick and fluffy (because I tie them), and they can go into washing machines to be scrubbed clean until they are worn to pieces, in which case, I will make new ones. This kind of quilt is, of course, a comforter.

Making it was great fun. It took just three days to make the top, cutting the pieces with my rotary cutter and stitching them so fast it seemed that my sewing machine would smoke. One quilt has big red block letters that read "Jonathan," surrounded with red, starry-looking Farmer's Daughter blocks. For the backing, I found a piece of gaudy red and white material at the store on a pile of flat-fold fabrics. The fabric is printed with the words "Go Big Red," which is an ideal fabric for a three-year-old Nebraska boy who goes to sports events with his parents.

I loved putting that quilt top together. It was easy to cut every block meticulously and to stitch it speedily and accurately. Each block was a perfect measurement and a perfect square shape. I set the quilt top together quickly, ironing it flat and smooth. Last night, it was ready to be backed, padded, and tied.

I lay out the backing on the floor, straight and even. I spread the quilt top on top of it right sides together, matching the edges. The flat, perfect, smooth quilt top turned renegade. It rippled and rumpled. It was as uneven as a bowl of popcorn. Each time I make a quilt, I come to this moment of accounting. It can be a quick and easy quilt top for a comforter like this one, or it can be a top for a treasure quilt that has taken me several years of patient piecing to complete. However I make it, when I lay it out, it suddenly goes all out of control.

If I put the layers together traditionally, spreading the backing, batting, and top, and basting heavily, or if I quick-assemble the pieces, no matter what method, no matter the effort, at this point the top asserts its own wayward personality.

My first reaction when I reach this point in my quiltmaking is always one of despair. I tend to panic, and then I remember the Magic. I remember that somehow, some way, all those hundreds of little pieces, cut in a myriad of different directions, will slowly lie down flat and even. They will conform. If I can keep my cool and be patient, my quilt top will turn from a pumpkin into a beautiful being.

So, what did I do with this red Jonathan quilt? I pinned the edges together with lots of pins. Then, I stitched around them leaving an opening of about eighteen inches. I laid it back down on the floor, smoothing it as best I could, and I

- - - -

spread the batting on top, pinned it around the edges, and sewed around it again.

The next step is one that my husband, Bill, loves to watch because I look so absurd when I do it. I laid the whole kit and kaboodle on the floor again, and wrestled with it, slowly inverting it, pulling the bulk through that opening. Then, exhausted and perspiring, I pinned the opening together and stitched it on the machine. I made a second circuit around the outside, top stitching it to give the edges some sort of definition.

All of this takes a lot of faith. I remind myself that I have cut and pieced this blob accurately and that in spite of the fact that the whole mess looks like an utter catastrophe at this point, I must believe in it. Slowly, I ease the swollen hump of fluff into shape on the floor, smoothing, patting, stretching, shifting, and slowly the Magic happens. Who was the woman, do you suppose, who first faced a quilt in progress, and knew, deep in her heart, that if she trusted and persevered, all those lumps and bumps would turn into a smooth, even quilt?

Now it is finished, a cheerful comforter that is perfect to cuddle a three-year-old boy. "Oh," I will tell my friends when they see it and applaud, "It was just one of those quick things that I do. I gave it a slap and a bang, and it just whipped together." Those people will say the same thing they always say to me. "Helen, you are amazing. You do these things so easily!"

Of course! Abracadabra!

Slow and Steady Wins the Race

Every year, Bill and I go to a folk festival in a small Iowa town. For three days, we celebrate. We eat delicious foods piled with sugar and cinnamon and whipped cream, we sit on the curb in the sunshine to watch the marchers and horses and floats parade down the street, and we dance old-time polkas and waltzes by starlight. We watch folk dancers in front of the courthouse and we admire crafts and quilts in the school gymnasium.

Each year, we enjoy this adventure, and each year, Bill likes to try something new and different. This year, he decided that he would hike the 5-K walk/race along the river. We got to the starting line early Saturday morning. The dew was heavy on the grass, and the heat had not yet begun to simmer across the striped awnings of the food booths. The area was filled with hikers and runners. They all seemed to be athletic and muscular. All of them were in shorts. Some shorts were cut high on the thighs. Some wore form-fitting lycra pants that hugged tiny hips and fannies. The runners represented a wide variety of ages, though most of them were young and lean. The older people in the crowd, however, showed tight, strong sinews in the calves of their bare legs. The young men were a gleaming, bronze color. The young women were taut, firm, and fit.

The runners exercised. They stretched their muscles. They bent down to reach the ground, their toes, their heels. It was a well-rehearsed ritual. Muscles rippled.

There was a moment of quiet as the loudspeaker gargled out directions—"Runners in front, walkers in the rear," and suddenly, the crowd surged forward down the street. Bill brought up the rear dressed in his everyday jeans and wearing his battered gardening hat.

In another moment the street was empty and quiet. I waited in the car. I sewed, in fact, on my little quilt. In time, people began to drift back across the finish line. They sparkled with perspiration. It was an hour before Bill appeared. His number flapped bravely on his back. His shoulders were damp, but he was triumphant. He was, he said, at least not the last person.

As Bill had set out among the hundreds, he had set a goal, he said. He had decided that he would pass each person ahead of him, one at a time. Each time he passed another hiker, he felt a small triumph. He said it took him a mile to pass the lady with the baby carriage. Bill finished his race, and he was not the first or the second or among the leaders, but he did finish it with his head high and with each step a new success.

I feel the same way about this quilt I am making. It has forty-eight blocks. I planned small blocks that would measure only eight inches because I reasoned that half-size blocks would be half the work of large blocks. Let me tell you now that, no matter the size, forty-eight blocks ARE forty-eight blocks. I began this quilt bravely. I believed that I would whip out the blocks in jig time, making a few stitches here and a few cuts there. I quickly discovered that every step was a challenge, every block a new success. The trick to success is to keep my eye ahead, my mind intent on "passing the lady with the baby carriage." I have sixteen blocks finished. Now, I must make block number seventeen and then another step and another. Eventually, I will "pass the baby carriage."

To hear me talk, you would not believe that I am actually enjoying the making of these blocks. I simply didn't calculate the quilting mathematics accurately. If I can make four blocks today, orange blossoms and lilacs, I will be four steps further along in this race. I can make four more tomorrow, perhaps violets and roses. Look out, lady with the baby carriage, because I am going to be passing you at any moment. Every quilt block I make will be another step along the route, and when I cross that finish line, I'll have something better than a medal or a trophy. I'll have a quilt.

Gaining a New Dimension

I have been given a gift. I have heard about classes in learning to listen, a skill they are teaching people who believe they already know how to hear. I have heard about epicures "sharpening their palates," meaning that they are learning to taste discriminately. Now I have entered into a new world. Ever since our daughter, Connie, lost her sight, we have been working with her to help her learn the art of "living without sight." I find that I am doing a strange thing. Sometimes I inadvertently close my eyes in a sort of empathy when I am working beside her. There, in this new world, is a sort of awareness I have never known before.

Like you, I am a quilter. I've always thought that I am a quilter because I am a tactile person. I like to feel things. When I go to a quilt show, I have to clasp my hands behind my back to control them. Still, many times I have reached out to touch the forbidden fruit when a member of the white-glove patrol has turned her back. Now I find a truth about myself. I have hardly begun to understand the enjoyment at my fingertips.

For instance, let's take ice. What does ice feel like? It's cold, of course. But isn't it more than that? It may be slippery. It may be runny wet. It may grow perceptibly smaller in your fingers. It may be sharp or smooth. It may be so cold that it is painful. It may even be so cold that it is sticky. There is ice-cube ice and the kind of ice you find on the inside wall of

- - - -

your freezer. There is the thin skin of ice you find covering your car in October or mushy ice that melts in your driveway in April. There is the sharp, brittle ice of twenty degrees below zero, or rough, battered ice on a frozen lake. And, of course, there is slippery, slithery ice that melts off the ice-cube compartment when you defrost. If there are that many kinds of ice to feel, what an incredible world of textures lies untouched at our fingertips.

As quilters, we can feel weaves and quilting stitches and surface finishes. There are quilts with flannel surfaces and thick, fluffy batts. What about the crispy feeling of an old quilt that has just been washed? Hang it on the clothesline; blow it in the wind! Make it soft for your cheek at night. Old cotton batt quilts covered with delicate stitches have a gentle thinness. Long quilting stitches have a thready quality. Tiny stitches dimple a polyester batt. A flannel-batt quilt has an unforgiving, heavy weight.

The gift I have received is the discovery that I can enrich my life by teaching myself to use, really use, my sense of touch. The pleasure of feeling is a sense to be cultivated. This awareness is adding a whole new dimension to my quilts and to my life.

Eating Humble Pie

Well, I did it! I did it good. I went and broke my thumb. It was my own fault. I was stupid. I was careless. If I could blame the accident on a pet, or a friend, or an Act of God, it would not be so embarrassing. As it was, purely and simply, I slammed my own hand in a car door.

My right thumb is crushed, and I am totally right-handed. My hand looks like Little Jack Horner's with a giant plum on it where my thumb is. It is large and round, and it sticks straight up in the air. It is hard to hide a large, bandaged thumb, and I believe that I can say unequivocally that my friends (and a few strangers) who have seen it have told me every gruesome horror story about thumbs ever imagined.

Some things in my life are still possible. I can drive, move furniture, and fold laundry without my thumb. Without my thumb, I can cook a meal, read a book, and even take a shower, if I keep my thumb dry by holding it over my head. I can brush my teeth, but I am awkward, and the toothpaste runs down my arm and drips from my elbow. I can do all this without using my thumb. However, I am suffering emotional stress from this whole affair, and I need comfort. This morning, I decided to try sewing. Over the years, I've given lots of advice (much of it unsolicited) to quilters with hand problems. I've told them how to deal with arthritis, carpal tunnel syndrome, and tendonitis. Mostly, I've said blithely, "Try it a different way. Retrain! Change the pattern of your work." Ha!

The doctor was gloomily encouraging. "You may eventually be able to get your scissors over that thumb," he said. Undaunted, I experimented with my various scissors and discovered that I can indeed get my thumb (bandage and all) through the hole in my largest pair. Even better, I found that, if I don't exert any pressure on my thumb, I can hold my rotary cutter in my fist quite successfully. So, I can cut. That's the first hurdle.

Now, the sewing machine. With a little patience, a considerable amount of fiddling, and a few strong words, I found that I could grasp the electrical plug, direct it, and fit it into the wall outlet. Threading the machine was fairly simple. Inserting my bobbin into my machine was a different story. Without my thumb, I couldn't feel the little, pointy projection on the top of the bobbin case to orient it. The bobbin jammed in the hook race. It stuck. Under other circumstances, I would simply have released the hook race, removed the bobbin, and reinserted it. All of the platitudes, all of the breeziness with which I had treated others problems came home to roost. The problem seemed bigger than a simple "try it a new way." I knew that, if I released it, I quite probably would not be able to get it back into the machine with my ping pong-paddle-like thumb.

I would have told someone else to put the work away and come back tomorrow, when things would undoubtedly go more smoothly. My tomorrow is probably four months away. I need to sew now. To fix my machine, I got down on my knees and peered up into its depths. I jiggled and I poked. Luckily, the bobbin fell out. I wound it full of thread and, eventually, I tumbled it back into place correctly. I am not looking forward to running out of thread and repeating the process.

I have been sewing all morning, slowly, and I have discovered: A person does not need a thumb to use a seam ripper, or to iron, and can carefully push in pins with the tip of a bandaged finger. A person without the use of a thumb will have difficulty knotting a thread for hand sewing, but with patience, that person can stitch on a sewing machine.

I have learned that there is many a slip between the lip and the rip (of a needle). It is easy to give advice; it is harder to take it. Next time I get Pollyanna-ish about others' handicaps and frustrations, I will try to insert a bobbin without using my thumb. I will try to pick up pins, draw patterns, or shuffle papers wearing mittens. I will try to use my scissors with my left hand. I will remind myself what it is like to work with fingers that do not function properly. If I fumble with my own ineptness, perhaps it will help me to deal more kindly with others who are struggling with handicaps. Until now, I have sympathized, but I have not truly understood. I am learning patience from this experience, I am learning gratitude for what I can do. And I am learning humility.

Life Is a Sandwich

While eating lunch with quilting friends, I was seated at a large, round table near a sunny window. I opened my provided box lunch. Inside was a bag of potato chips, a large, gooey cookie, and a sandwich. Not just any sandwich. This sandwich took my breath away. The bread was homemade, brown, freshly soft, and sliced at least an inch thick. Between two of these delicious slabs of bread was a large, fresh, green leaf of lettuce and a gigantic scoop of chicken salad, chunky with meat and rich with mayonnaise.

"How," I wondered to myself, "am I ever going to get my mouth around that?"

I debated for a few minutes. The quilters around me were tackling the problem with forks, proceeding with great poise.

"Perhaps," I reasoned, "I could handle this like a grilled cheese sandwich. If I compress it, I could get a better grip on it. The sandwich, then being thinner, could be squeezed into my mouth."

I pressed the palm of my hand on the top of the entire concoction. The bread did indeed compact. Also, the chicken and mayonnaise oozed between my fingers and dribbled out. While everyone around me ate their sandwiches with utensils in mannerly perfection, I licked my fingers and chased the errant remnants of the salad down the front of my clothing. My sandwich was out of control.

And so is this project that I am working on now.

- - - -

I am making a quilt that requires bits and pieces of odd materials. I bought dozens of quarter yards of "thing" fabrics printed with small objects on them. I came home with fat, lazy, cats, tiny cheater quilt fabric, and fabric with flowerpots. My new quilt will have windows, lots of windows, and I am creating rooms behind them where patchwork people will live and laugh.

When I began working on this quilt, I thought I could control this array of fat quarters, I intended to look through all of it, piece by piece, cutting out my windows precisely and stacking them neatly so that I would be able to make easy choices. I wanted to be able to sort through my cut-out windows much as if I were going to a cafeteria, picking this and that for my quilt "feast." There would be no scraps and no loose threads scattered across my workroom. I was organized, and it would all be very neat and orderly and proper.

I searched my quarter yards of material, cutting rectangular holes in them here and there, building wonderful fantasies in my mind as I worked of fabric windows with furniture and people. I planned a fabric quilt shop with displays of sewing baskets. For the fruit shop, I found fabric with crates of cherries and a basket of oranges. I found fragrant, steaming pies to cool on the windowsills at the bakery. I cut my patchwork windows neatly, spewing relatively few pieces of fabric on the floor around me.

I remembered, as I worked, unexplored fabrics in my stash. I began pulling out hoarded scraps and cutting into them, I paused only briefly to pull a few clinging threads off my clothing. This game was great fun.

I began to dig heedlessly, strewing snippets. I found fabric for a stationery store and a whole party of tiny quilters sitting around a quilt frame. I cut deliriously, I dribbled shreds, I spilled cuttings.

As my stack of patchwork windows grew, so did the debris. The scraps multiplied, the color spilled across my floor. I found the discoveries intriguing, the texture delectable. I savored old thoughts and brand new ideas. I splashed in my pile of fabric. I tasted the joy of puttering. Threads cascaded down the front of my clothes, and like my chicken salad, I found the excitement spilling and spreading. It was nourishing. It was satisfying. It was delicious.

Chapter 2

KEEPING US
IN STITCHES

A Matter of Policy

My husband has an appointment with an insurance agent tomorrow. I will go along as usual. However, I expect that this conference will be different from past experiences.

Usually, I go along and sit, nodding my head and looking intense, as if I am absorbing the whole conversation and making difficult decisions. In truth, I am mentally plotting the border design for my next quilt. What makes tomorrow's meeting different is that I shall go knowing what insurance is all about. I have learned the lingo. When I realized that this meeting was coming up, I made a personal commitment to study and learn the mysteries of the insurance world. I got out the books and the old policies, and I studied. I am prepared. It was not difficult after all.

For those of you who have struggled with the intricacies of insurance jargon, I have prepared a glossary to simplify your life. You, too, can become an expert!

- *limited coverage*: a crib quilt
- *extended coverage*: a king-size quilt
- *fidelity bond*: a wedding quilt
- *workman's compensation*: two quilts
- *premium*: a Friendship Quilt
- *disability*: a sore finger
- *high risk*: buying just enough fabric to piece out the last block of your quilt

- *li-ability*: no puckers, no lumps
- *benefits*: (translated from the Latin) *bene*: good, *fits*: at the center points of your star
- *endowment*: when your best friend cleans out her fabric cupboard
- *adjuster*: the husband who tucks the quilt around him until you are left with one shoulder and one leg out in the cold
- *interest rate*: that which declines with your husband the longer the quilt frame stands in the middle of the living room floor
- *a-gent*: a husband who never complains
- *straight life*: not the Drunkard's Path
- *social security*: Hand of Friendship
- *underwriter*: one who signs her quilt in the lower left- or right-hand corner
- *grace period*: when all is stitched and done, the time to stand back and admire

Oh, Say Can You See?

Optometrists are interesting people. They believe with all sincerity that because they went to school for years and years and studied highly technical courses, they know everything there is to know about glasses. I suppose they do.

However, I had an argument with my optometrist. The one thing he doesn't know about is how I want my glasses. I went in for my checkup. I hadn't had my eyes examined for several years, and I decided that when I could no longer see to thread my needle, it was time for a change. I wear bifocals, big ones. I want to see my quilting. Just as I had hoped, the doctor announced that a stronger prescription would solve my vision problems. We discussed my quilt. He determined that my glasses should focus at lap height, just right for a book.

"No," I said firmly, "I want it about this high."

I raised my arms bust high and indicated a line at the level between my right arm and a slightly lower left arm. You guessed it! It was right at quilt-frame height. We argued a bit—quite a bit. I told him that the most important thing in the world is that I see my quilt frame. I cannot move the frame closer or adjust its height. I can move books, needles, lights, anything else, but not my quilt frame.

My optometrist has always thought (politely) that I was a goofy lady. Maybe I am. He has known me for years. But on this day I was very firm about my requirements.

Now I have my new glasses. They focus beautifully on my quilt frame. My stitches are small and clear. I love my work.

Life at the quilt frame is all that I thought it should be.

And now, I can no longer read labels on quilts at quilt shows. I can no longer read name tags pinned to lapels of would-be friends—if I could only see their names without bending down in an embarrassing way until their chests are at quilt-frame distance from my glasses. I cannot sign checks at the check-out stands at the grocery store gracefully. When I walk, I stumble over steps in odd places, humps in carpets, and suitcases.

If I told my optometrist this, he would chuckle. He knew this would happen. But what he didn't know is that when I quilt, there is joy. My eyes are sharp; my work is neat. The world is glorious through my magic glasses.

"All My Problems" (A Soap Opera)

Can a one-armed stitcher find happiness in a world where everyone quilts—or wishes she did, or ought to? I was rushing to the back door last night when suddenly the dog loomed up in front of me. I did a magnificent swan dive over her back and landed with a great splat in the middle of the kitchen floor. I lay there a moment and regained my senses. I took inventory. Almost everything that should move, did. My toes, my legs, my head. Then I knew that I had "done it." My left arm was definitely strange. It did not do the things that left arms are supposed to do. I had most certainly broken it.

As a quilter, my thoughts were not, "How will I take care of my grandchildren on their three-day visit?" I did not worry how I would cook or scrub. I could relinquish that job to others. The thoughts that went through my mind were something like this:

"How will I drive to that quilt meeting tomorrow? I suppose if I drive with my right hand, I can hook my left fingers around the wheel, and I can let the damaged arm rest in my lap.

"How will I get through the airport to that quilt convention I have dreamed about for so long? I have my big, blue scrap-bag. I have my little suitcase with my small quilts for Show and Tell. There is the big suitcase that trots along behind me on wheels and my purse filled with playing cards, crossword puzzle books, airsick pills, combs, checkbooks, and my latest quilting project. If I go girded as for crossing the Alps, how will I manage?

"How can I quilt? For a whole month I have promised myself to work on my new project next week. Can I baste it? Can I catch it between my knees to hold it and stitch with it on my lap? Can I thread my needle long-distance?"

Now I am in the strange, new world of a handicapped quilter. I am eating all of the platitudes I have uttered when other quilters have said, "I'm having such problems—my arthritis won't let me use my hands the way I used to," or "I can't see to thread this needle anymore." I have always said, with sympathy, "Then let's find a new, a different way."

Now *I* shall have to find different, new ways.

First, I must decide what is important and what is not. There is no way that I can open a stuck peanut butter jar or a childproof pill bottle with one hand. That is not important. The child can do that. Dressing myself is a consideration, if only to keep my self-respect. I can button my skirt in the front and then twist it around to the back. This leaves me with a decidedly rumpled appearance and my blouse spiraling around my torso, but it is adequate.

The nitty-gritty, the important things in life, I am discovering, can be licked. My fingers still work. I can thread my needle by guess and by golly. I can sew seams that do not require really fine stitching. I can baste. I can pin. I can prop my arm up on my sewing machine table and stitch to my heart's content.

– – – –

The family will run, tote, and scrub. Friends will drop by with cool drinks and comforting advice. This is, in truth, a time of wealth, of solicitude.

"And so, dear reader, as Helen faces this new episode in her life, will she finish blind stitching the binding onto her miniature pieced quilt? Will her appliqué lie smooth, her curves gentle and sweeping? Will Helen's bedroom dresser recover after being decorated with four colors of crayon by her three-year-old granddaughter during the time when Helen was writing these reflections?"

Curses, Foiled Again

Ordinarily, I am not a profane woman. I am a fairly toler-ant and accepting person. Is it profanity to curse something when you really mean it? That's what I did this morning.

I had been to the fabric shop. It was a store where I had never shopped before and the clerk's antennae went up the moment I walked in the door. What is there about me that alerts store clerks, that sets them salivating? It can't be my bulging purse. There is little money in it, only my thimble, a pair of scissors, several spools of thread, my lipstick, and my checkbook. This morning I had instant service in that store. In fact, I believe the clerk left another customer to help me. I poked into fabric. I pulled out bolts. I unwound whole lengths of material. It was wonderful. I carried fabrics over to the shop window to see them come alive in natural light. I fingered texture between my thumb and forefinger. I laid out fabrics to see how the colors played together.

The clerk climbed ladders to reach the high bolts. She carried armfuls of fabrics for me to see. Her instincts were right. By the time I had finally made my choice, I had bought all of it, a whole bolt of it. It was a lovely chintz splashed with apple blossoms and butterflies. I hope my friends love that fabric, too, because I have so much of it; enough even that the clerk offered to carry it to my car for me.

- - - -

There, now, sat my fabric in the back of my car, wrapped in a paper printed with an old calico design. The sun shone on it through the back window. The day was so lovely that I rolled down the window and breathed deeply as I backed my car out of the parking lot. I drove into the street and stopped at the red light. The light changed to green. Suddenly, my car was frozen in its tracks. The gearshift refused to budge. I jiggled it; I shook it; I banged it. The cars behind blew at me. I turned and peered at them beyond my bulging package and waved frantically for them to pass me. I cursed my car. My trouble light blinked rhythmically. The cars pulled around me one by one. Only the thought of my wonderful package sustained me.

I struggled again with my gearshift. On similar occasions in the past, the repair people have told me that I don't have an actual problem. They have suggested that I should learn how to drive my car. When all else has failed, they have gone to the extreme of suggesting that perhaps I should replace my battery! Ridiculous! I am tired of arguing with repairmen. I thought up a new curse.

Underneath my lovely, calico-wrapped parcel was a screwdriver. I shifted the bundle and extricated it. I pried at my gearshift. I thumped it. It yielded slightly. It slid into second gear and locked in place. My stubborn car hesitantly started in second gear. It began to move and then achieved the dreary speed of 20 m.p.h. I was not a happy woman, but I was, indeed, moving. I needed comforting. I pulled my bundle of fabric onto the seat beside me. It nestled reassuringly against my leg.

Slowly I made my way across town, my right wheels on the shoulder of the road. Passing drivers peered at me with curiosity, wondering if I was a timid, little old lady out for a "drive." I patted my bundle of fabric. Its nearness calmed me. An interminable time later I slid the car into the parking space in front of my house. I uttered a few more oaths at it and, cradling my package of fabric, I retreated to the house.

We are home, my fabric and I. It is a lovely fabric. The butterflies glide gently around the pastel flowers. Now and again they alight. Getting my fabric home, however, was not lovely. I discovered that I have a versatile vocabulary. I have never fully appreciated it before, and I am not sure what I have done to my car.

Have I put a curse on it, a curse surely like the curse of Old Tut's tomb? Is my car doomed to steady deterioration? Will the wheels fall off? Will it dissolve into rust? Will it wheeze and expire?

Perhaps the ritual of snipping my soft, new fabric into pieces and blending it with other warm, wonderful colors will produce a suitable gentleness of spirit to undo any profane damage I have done. Perhaps the sweet charm of my patchwork will work its healing wonders.

– – – –

Consider the Lilies

I fell down again. Well, almost, sort of. I had been sitting on the roof of my garage all morning, photographing a quilt. It was a big one, and I was shooting straight down because my stepladder wasn't tall enough to get above the quilt and get all of it into the picture. Besides, standing on the ladder, my shadow kept getting into the picture. Anyhow, I had grown quite casual about heights and sure-footedness, and I felt invincible.

Down the alley my neighbor had a flock of lovely daylilies growing up against her garage, glowing in the sun. "Wouldn't it be lovely," I thought, "to hang my quilt behind those lilies and photograph them in all of their gloriousness!"

Down the alley I trooped, if you can call one grandmother and one granddaughter a "troop." I carried my ladder and a long pole and some pushpins and some molding hooks and The Quilt.

I unfolded the ladder and clambered up. The top step has a sign on it. The sign says, "Do not stand on this step." I never pay any attention to this sign.

I leaned over against the roof edge of my neighbor's garage. Carefully I unfolded the quilt and let it drop down behind the lilies, all golden and red and leafy. I held the long pole with my left hand, leveling the quilt that was pinned to it. With my right hand, I reached out to hang the pole on a molding hook I had placed on the roof edge.

- - - -

The ladder shifted under my feet. It moved. It actually backed up. There I was suspended horizontally with my white fingertips clutching the edge of the garage roof and my toetips on the far-away top of the ladder step that said, "Do not stand on this step."

Now, the point of this story is not that I shouted while my grandchild raced between the houses of my neighbors until she found a steady pair of shoulders to stand beneath me and help me support myself while I climbed down. Indeed, my neighbor was swift and strong and understanding.

And the point is not that you should read and obey signs, which I should have done.

The point is that my lovely quilt fell down among those daylilies, and in that moment of foolishness, you cannot imagine the damage that was done. All of the reading I have done about natural dyes and flower colors did not prepare me for that disaster. In one swift moment, my pristine quilt was covered with brilliant yellow from the stamens of the gold lilies, purple from the red lilies, and green from the foliage. I went into shock.

Back I went to my house and sat and stared at my quilt-of-many-colors. What was a person to do? When I had recovered sufficiently to think straight, I got out that little booklet I had bought one day at the grocery check-out, the one I paid 35¢ for and tells all about stain removal. That purchase was one of my luckier impulses. It had gotten me out of many a mess before. I looked up "flowers" in the index among "coffee stains" and "chocolate." Apparently nobody else drops things into lily beds. There was no "flowers." I remembered then that I have always removed fruit stains from my Christmas tablecloth with boiling water. It was worth a try.

Four pots full of boiling water and one burned-up hotpad later I had removed some spots. Back I went to the book, remembering, this time, that "grass" is a foliage, and sure enough, I found a recommendation, the first for alcohol, and the second, peroxide. I was willing to risk the alcohol, but not the peroxide. Four more pots of water went onto the stove, and I set myself up with a bottle of rubbing alcohol and an old toothbrush.

It all came out in the end. I saved my quilt. But the big thing I remembered about the whole affair was my blessing for the person who had made my quilt. She had washed her fabric before she had made the quilt.

People ask me if I wash my fabric before I make a quilt, and I always answer, "I should, but I usually don't. I get so excited that I usually just plunge in." If that fabric in The Quilt had not been prewashed, I could never on this green earth have poured all of that goop into it and had it come out colorfast and unshrunk and wonderfully like new. Bless that quiltmaker. Always now, when I am preparing to make a quilt, my fabric will first of all go into the washing machine. I will always consider the lilies.

– – – –

Bow Wow

I made a quilt lining yesterday. It was big and pieced with a lot of pieces, I had the idea to make this fancy lining for the new quilt top that I had just finished. I knew it was going to be wonderful.

I woke early yesterday and washed and pressed the fabrics I had chosen—two colors that were so powerful that I knew they needed some relief. But I reasoned that this was a lining and, therefore, it should complement the front instead of competing with it. The colors were, after all, two of the same colors used on the completed quilt top, so they should work well together.

The next thing I did was to hunt up a picture of a Garden Maze lattice design. The pattern was easy to draft, just three 2″-wide strips with a cross on either end. It was a snap to map it out on graph paper.

I measured the borders on the top so that I wouldn't have the lining seams falling at the same place. Oh, this was going to be just great! I took out my rotary cutter and cutting board, and I had a cup of coffee. I chopped out perfect little rectangles and squares with my cutter and pinned them together. My sewing machine hummed. Along about noon, I ate my cup of yogurt and a peanut butter sandwich.

When the family came home for supper, I was astonished. How could it be almost six o'clock? I ran to the store for

_ _ _ _

corn and zucchini and whipped up a quick meal in between sewing-machine and ironing-board sessions. Then, I had another cup of coffee.

To be social, I took my pinning and my ripping into the living room during the evening while the family watched TV. By bedtime I only had the borders left. It was time to turn in.

Around three o'clock in the morning, I admitted to myself that I wasn't going to sleep until I had sewn on those last four pieces—the two side borders and the top and bottom. The job took only half an hour. Now I could sleep.

This morning, in the light of day, I examined my new quilt lining. The points are perfect, the intersections meet precisely. The measurements are exact. It lies flat.

I hate it!

It's wrong, all wrong. The design is too big, too clumsy to go with my lovely quilt top. The colors are garish. Somehow they worked on the front but not on the lining. Rather than making my finished quilt something that would be exciting to turn over and discover what was on the back, it would, instead, make someone ask. "Why in heaven's name did she ever do that?" It is ugly.

I can live with the fact that I invested a whole day on this "monster," this "dog." I could have spent a lot more time, but how do I reconcile my conscience about the money I spent on five yards of fabric? Obviously, I will have to go back to the quilt store and see if they have five more yards of the border fabric so that I can make a solid lining. It's just that I have this green and hot pink "beast" sitting here shaking its finger at me, making me wonder what I can ever do with it.

Perhaps there is someone in a nursing home or a church sewing circle who would like to use it as a quilt top. Only, I would feel guilty foisting it on some unsuspecting, innocent soul. My thriftiness won't let me throw it away, and I don't need one more quilt top to store here in my workroom, certainly not one I hate so much. I need this thing out of my house.

Friday is guild-meeting day. There will be 150 tasteful, clever quilters there. They are creative people, and, what's more, they like challenges.

Ah, my mind is working this all out now. By George, I've got it! Here's my approach. This is what I'm going to say: "Dear friends, everyone is making challenge quilts these days. Some challenges ask what a quilter can do with a particular fabric. Some challenges ask what a quilter can do with a pattern or a special size or a subject. This is a new and different challenge. What can you do with an ugly quilt? All answers will be considered fairly and expeditiously. The grand-prize winner might, of course, be lucky enough to get this remarkable, colorful, big quilt thing."

Don't you think it's a great idea? I could be rid of the "brute" forever knowing that it had to live at someone else's house. The only trouble with the idea is, do you drink anyone will risk winning the prize?

- - - -

Seams Like Old Times

I bought a blouse. I was vacationing in another country, and I saw a raspberry pink blouse in a shop. I wasn't sure what size to buy. Usually I buy a size 10. If the price on the item is embarrassingly costly and the fit is looser, I will even buy a size 8. The salesclerk in the store was a young girl with a sweet, innocent face, who looked over my body and said, "They run small. You'd be wise to get a larger size." They had no 12's, so I bought a raspberry blouse in size 14.

Back home, I opened my package. I tried on my new blouse for the first time. It was enormous, large enough for two of me at once. I tried wearing it under my suit by pulling the excess fabric around to the back and yanking it down at the waist to make a smoother fit in the front. The neckline plunged well into the obscene zone. The lapels bunched and ruffled. The collar rippled. I could not run back to the store across the sea and exchange my blouse for a smaller size.

I have not sewn a garment in years. When I learned to make quilts, I vowed I would never again adjust a bust dart, ease in the top of a sleeve, or buttonhole anything.

I went out yesterday and bought a size 10 pattern for a traditional blouse without a yoke, exactly like the raspberry blouse. I sat last night with my seam ripper and removed endless overcast seams. Once I had the blouse in pieces, I ironed and recut them, using the right-size pattern pieces. This morning I have been sitting at my sewing machine reassembling them.

- - - -

Do you remember the women you have met who are beginning quilters, but who have told you quite positively that you can't tell them anything about quilting because they have been sewing all of their lives? I am a lady who thought you didn't need to tell her about sewing because she has been quilting for so many years. I discovered that when you use a ⅝″ seam, there is enough seam allowance fabric that it looks like a ruffle, In fact, my machine is so accustomed to ¼″ seams that I even had to sew a line on a test fabric to find out where ⅝″ was.

I do not own a serger. I assumed that I was never again going to make a blouse, and therefore, I didn't need one. I wish I had one, if only for today. I have been trench seaming this morning, tidying those scruffy edges—seam, trim, invert, press, seam. I had forgotten what sewing a blouse is like.

When I piece my quilts, the fabric pieces flow through the machine. I gang-stitch, feeding them through without even breaking a thread, piece after piece after piece, rather like a waltz. Pressing my quilting work makes it lie flat and even. A blouse is not supposed to lie flat since my body is not flat.

Now that my blouse is finished and I will be more re-spectably clad, I shall do some piecing this afternoon. It will be a relief to know exactly what to expect of my machine and my fabric. It will be wonderful. Remaking my raspberry blouse was a learning experience. The blouse fits but it is not a masterpiece.

I shall go back to my quilting with a new respect for dressmakers. I have always been smug about the fact that, though a person may know how to sew, quilting is a very specialized art. I now appreciate that, though I know how to quilt, sewing is not at all as easy as I remembered. With this hard lesson learned, I expect that I will continue to buy clothing at the discount store and keep on finding my happiness in quilting.

The Night That Time Stood Still

It had been a good day. Things seemed to go exactly right. The sun shone in a flawless sky in a flawless moment. Fortune smiled on me. During the morning, I found a long-lost letter behind a pile of fabric in my workroom. Then, as I pieced, my stitches were tiny and even, and my color choices lighted up my quilt and worked out just as I had imagined them in my mind's eye. As I worked, I sang along with the *Camelot* music on my CD player. Life was good.

Supper at night was easy, leftover stew reheated in the microwave, a chunk of lettuce for salad, and ice cream for dessert. I piled the dirty dishes in the sink, and left them. Later in the evening, I heard Bill moving about, cleaning up the kitchen. I was working without interruption, and my quilt was falling into place so perfectly that I hated to put it down. I promised myself that I would sew until ten o'clock, when the news came on the TV, and then I would put away my quilt and go to bed.

I smoothed out my freshly washed fabric and snipped and shaped more pieces. The work seemed effortless. It hardly seemed possible that I was working on my last block. How could anything go together so perfectly? The clock read ten minutes before nine.

More pressing and shaping for this final block. I glanced at the clock again, and it read ten minutes before nine. Do you

- - - -

remember the old "Twilight Zone" shows on television? The ones in which time was suspended? In those shows, suddenly all the world stood still, and the actor remembered old experiences or he saw into the future. Time slipped by, disembodying him. I, too, felt freed, floating, moving in my own, separate world, as if this perfect day would never end.

Bill called to me to tell me that he was going to bed. I glanced at the clock again—ten minutes before nine. It was strange that he should be going to bed so early. Maybe he had a morning appointment the next day. I ironed, and I shaped more fabric pieces. My work was flowing past me.

Eventually, I stopped long enough to go into the kitchen for a coffee break. As I stood sipping from the steaming cup, I glanced at the kitchen clock. It read three o'clock. How could this be? I checked my workroom clock again—ten minutes before nine. My workroom clock had died.

In that moment, I made a discovery. What I discovered was this: On that day, I had been given a gift of free, unencumbered time. I had not felt the pressures of meal planning or the frustrations of interruptions. I had not been burdened with the sensationalism and drama on the evening news report. I hadn't been driven by the relentless whirling of the clock hands. Instead, I had worked in a module of free and undisturbed quiet. I had simply existed here, quietly, without stresses or distraction. The gift was one of a perfect moment, one that I will never have again—because, sadly, I have become wise. Next time, when the clock stands still, I will check its batteries.

- - - -

One Potato, Two Potato

I'll bring the mashed potatoes," I said. The whole family was planning a special meal. One person volunteered veggies, one a pie. My husband, Bill, offered to bring along some of his famous sourdough bread.

I am not fond of making mashed potatoes. I suppose it goes back to my childhood when my job for family feasts was to peel and boil the potatoes and then to sit all alone on the back steps with the big pot, mashing and mashing and mashing. Mashing potatoes is not my favorite thing to do. Last week, however, we discovered wonderful, prepared frozen mashed potato flakes at our grocery store. Bill made supper that night, and the potatoes were delicious.

"I'll bring the potatoes," I said, knowing that all I would have to bring was the plastic package of frozen flakes. We left early in the morning for the party. I took along my potato preparations: the flakes, a carton of milk, a fancy pottery bowl, and some paprika to dust tastefully on top of the hot, fluffy concoction.

Everyone arrived at the party carrying wonderful, fragrant foods. When the time was nearly right to call everyone to the table, I produced my meager supplies. I scanned the back of the package for directions, measured out the flakes into the bowl, added the milk, and popped it in the microwave.

The microwave beeped. I opened it and slid the steaming bowl out onto the table. I had produced potato soup! The liquid potatoes sloshed back and forth against the sides of the dish. The family roared with laughter. We deduced that, in my haste, I had misread the chart on the package. I had measured out potato flakes for two servings and added milk for the entire package.

I've made lots of potato-soup quilts, calculated in haste. I find plain old-fashioned arithmetic a chore, and I tend to breeze through it. I would much rather be shopping for the fabric, feeling it, cutting it up, and serving it back together. Almost always, in my hurry to get my little pattern pieces counted and computed, something short-circuits. The results of my carelessness are usually awesome.

Sometimes I buy so much that, when my quilt is finished, I have a considerable amount left over. Not to worry! The extra goes into my stash, which may be the reason I have such an enormous stash.

Sometimes, however, I short myself on fabric. That fabric is always a piece that, when I return to the store for more, they have just sold the last scrap. Impatience and shortsightedness force me to be creative. My creative coping has produced some unique sashing, strips, seams, and sets. I have used inserts of odd leftover fabrics, added unplanned design touches, and altered sizes and shapes.

All of this takes much more time than the few moments I would have spent calculating accurately. It is, however, a great deal more fun, and when people say to me, "How clever! How did you ever think to add that touch to your quilt?" I just smile and look very wise and say, "Oh, the idea just came to me one day!"

- - - -

My current potato-soup quilt is an easy challenge. When I bought the backing, I thought I had plenty of fabric. After getting it home, I discovered that I had only $\frac{1}{16}''$ to spare. Usually, I make the hanging sleeve out of the leftover backing material. This potato-soup problem should be fairly easy to solve. I should be able to find a substitute in my stash, but as I hunt, I realize anew that there is an incredible variety of whites and off-whites, and I have not a single match in my cupboard. A quilt sleeve seems such a little challenge. I can solve it by using some of my excess printed fabric from the quilt top. This time I am lucky.

It is always a shock when I discover that I have spent the grocery money on an incredible over-supply of an expensive fabric, or that I have shorted myself an inch or two of that special, exactly right material for my quilt. Hasty calculations may produce potato soup and unique quilt challenges. This is part of the fun of creating. With a little imagination and a bit of making-do, I can add chives and cheese from my cupboard, or greens and yellows from my stash, and with them, I can invent a dandy feast.

A Monumental Mess

The woman looked at me with a dreamy smile, and she uttered the platitude we have all heard so many times, "There is no such thing as an ugly quilt." "Oh, yes, there is," I said. "I just made it."

I cannot imagine how I ever thought I could sew a picture of a stony castle wall at night and have it be bright and romantic. The quilt is a portrait of Edinburgh Castle, lighted for the wonderful Scottish Festival. The scene is mounted in an oval border of red Stuart tartan plaid, and the drawbridge and road are made of a green Gordon tartan plaid. The quilt has twelve different gray fabrics. Gray seemed a normal color for rocks.

I worked feverishly on that quilt, because I wanted to preserve the memory of our exciting visit. My piecing was perfect, and just before I added the red tartan border, I framed my castle in a wide white oval to accentuate the drama of the occasion.

When I had finished my quilt top, I laid it down on the backing and batting to make my quilt sandwich. To my astonishment, the center scene billowed up off the batting like a Macy's Thanksgiving Day Parade balloon. How could this have happened? I had measured, basted, and stitched it precisely. Because I had no choice, I picked out every one of those little stitches that secured the castle scene to the frame. I smoothed the center down flat against the batting and spent several evenings reapplying it.

The layered quilt went into the frame. I quilted day and night. Sore fingers were a small price to pay for this beautiful quilt. When the last quilting stitch was in, I took the quilt out of the frame and bound it, perfectly. The woven lines of the tartan plaid were straight and even and flat. Oh, it was glorious.

I put the last stitch in the binding and laid the finished quilt on the floor for viewing.

It was dreadful. It was gray. The red tartan turned grayish. The green tartan turned grayish. All twelve grays were gray. It was so gray that all of my intricate, clever quilting was invisible. I suppose I should not have been surprised that a quilt depicting a pile of stones at night would be gray.

Well, I thought, I've put all this time into my quilt, I've got to fix it. I got out my embroidery floss to embroider a quilt that was supposed to have no embroidery. For three days, I outlined walls and parapets. Satisfaction always seemed just beyond reach. It needed just a little more here, and just a little more there, and more, and more.

Finally, the quilt appeared to be acceptable. I got ready to block my quilt, as I always do. I stretched my piece of fiberglass screening across my quilting frame, placed a fan underneath to move the air gently, and sprayed the quilt with distilled water. I patted the quilt flat, laid a ruler along the edges to be sure they were absolutely straight, and left the quilt to dry. It dried even, straight, and perfect.

I turned the quilt over. The prewashed red tartan had bled through to the back, staining the white back with scarlet blots.

- - - -

In desperation, I mixed a solution of bleach and water, and with a tiny paintbrush, I painted out the red stains. The bleach water erased the red blotches. The quilt was acceptable. I turned the quilt right side up, and as I watched, white bleach spots began to dimple the red tartan. I was beyond weeping.

Nothing more could hurt my quilt. Anything I could do would be an improvement. I sat myself down with my red Pigma pen and began inking in the white spots. At first, the red ink paled as it reacted to the bleach, but I inked it several times, and the red ink marks deepened to match the rich red of the surrounding fabric.

The quilt is done, now—red on top, white on the back, even and straight. My daughter Helen pointed out that, if you hold it up in a dark corner, the castle actually glows, which is what I had in mind in the first place, except that there are not many people who hang quilts in dark corners.

This quilt was to have been a glorious representation of laughter and joy. Even though it seemed doomed from the outset, I persisted. I am going to put my quilt safely away, because I might yet poke a hole in it or spill coffee on it.

All quilts are not beautiful. My quilt is not beautiful, but it is done!

Vocabulary Lesson

I was taking a nap, covered by one of my favorite quilts, when the phone rang. The man on the phone said, "Hello. I'd like to talk to you about stuccoing." I replied, "Thank you for calling, but our house has siding, and we like it very much."

"No, no," he said. "I mean, do you do stuccoing?"

"I'm not very good at concrete," I confessed. "Why do you ask?"

"Well, you're in the phone book under 'patchwork,'" said he.

When I hung up the phone, I curled back into my chair to resume my interrupted nap, but my mind refused to sleep. My head played over the curious conversation and the fact that someone, anyone, would think that "patchwork" could mean repairing houses.

You and I and the whole world must certainly know that "patchwork" is the sheer pleasure of sewing pieces of fabric together to make a quilt. What other possibilities could there be? How could someone define a patch as anything other than a part of a grand textile design?

There is, of course, that book about Mrs. Wiggs and her charming family in her cabbage patch, a patch that was a scrap of vegetable garden. If a car skids in the winter, we speak of it slipping on a patch of ice.

- - - -

What about patching up a quarrel? I suppose that, when we use "patch" that way, we are suggesting that we mend a rift in a friendship; putting it right, fixing it up, and making it whole again by adding a scrap of warmth and understanding.

Patches, I guess, can mean a lot of things that have to do with scraps of earth, or ice, or relationships, or fabric. Yet how very strange, that anyone could imagine that a patchworker is a person who splatters and daubs hard, rough cement.

And with that thought, my mind is gentled, and I put away thoughts of concrete, and I pull the shreds of my nap about me. I tuck my soft, warm patchwork quilt under my chin and I snooze.

Chapter 3
THE QUILT
CONNECTION

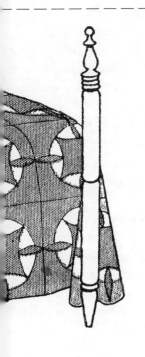

De-lightful! De-lovely!

My small quilt group met yesterday. I say that with some hesitation. The group is very small, little quilting was done, and the word "met" sounds pretty formal. What we did was, we got together, a few of us who indulge ourselves in total foolishness. We have known each other for a long time, but at this gathering we had a very serious discussion about what to call ourselves. After all, a name for the group would add a touch of validity and seriousness of purpose. We discussed all of the wonderful names that groups across this country have adopted, things like "Quilt Batts" and "Evening Bags" and "Blockheads" and we came to the unanimous decision that absolutely the only name appropriate for our group is "Idiots' Delight."

Taking a name after having existed in anonymity for several years was a good step.

To further validate our existence, we briefly considered electing officers. When it was proposed that height should be the qualification for president, our tallest member fell to her knees and instantly became the shortest person present. When you think about it, the prospect of becoming president of our group would turn us all into Toulouse-Lautrec look-alikes. Without a president, obviously a vice president is unnecessary. Since we do not propose to write letters or keep minutes and we have no money, a further slate of officers is unnecessary.

Over the last few years we have met on a regularly irregular basis—whenever, wherever, and however we felt was appropriate. The qualification for hostessing seems to be either a superior ability in the kitchen or a willingness to bring in carry-out refreshments from one of the local fast-food places. Cleanliness-of-house is not a requirement. In fact, at one of our last meetings, the hostess's house was given a careful white-glove inspection by two of the attendees. She did not pass muster.

Occasions for our meetings are varied, anything from a round-the-world trip bon-voyage party to merely wanting to show off a current quilt project.

Yesterday's gathering was a surprise birthday party for me. In my naiveté, I almost forgot it was my birthday. The women gathered with their quilting, though I was the only person who actually threaded a needle and took some stitches. There was a good deal of laying out of current projects on the carpet. This hostess had a clean floor. We ate too much, everything people our age aren't supposed to eat: tacos, potato chips and dip, cheese, and coffee . . . coffee . . . coffee. It was wonderful. The day ended with our departure by the basement door because our hostess had dead-bolted the front door and couldn't figure out how to re-open it. I went home to rest my ribs and facial muscles. I heard recently that it's the smiles that line our faces and maybe this group is the reason why I am so wrinkled.

Last night, I sat in my own living room quilting on my little white baby quilt and remembering the day. I decided that we must all meet here at my house same time next year to mark the passage of time from one momentous birthday to another. Therefore, I have written this letter:

Dear "Idiot,"

I am enclosing one delightful block. This is your challenge:

To each of you other "Idiots," I am sending one block and the pattern for this gorgeous star. I have kept one for myself. You are challenged to create another "Idiot's Star Block" and to send one to each of the rest of us sometime, any time before my next birthday, at which point in my life I will be older, fatter, grayer, and a better person.

On this historic and remarkable date next year, each of us "Idiots" will reveal a wall hanging comprised of the six "Idiot Stars," the likes of which nobody else in the world will have (or want).

Signed in awe and anticipation,
Helen

I have made six quilt blocks. They are simple Lemon Stars, but they are made with the diamonds of a wonderful fabric that says things like "Wow" and "Zowy" and there are streaks of lightning and squiggles. My stars are feather-stitched around the edges and there is a lovely button sewn right in the middle so that nobody but me knows if my points come together neatly or if there is a hole underneath. My six blocks are quite unique. Now, I shall slip each block into an envelope with a copy of the letter and send them off. I am not sure if I can stand waiting a year to get my own "Idiot Blocks" so that I can make some sort of wonderful wall hanging. The prospect of seeing five other hangings with the creations of these remarkable women will have me waiting breathlessly for this next year. In fact, when I host that extraordinary meeting, I may even clean my house (they can bring their white gloves), because I can't wait to be another year older.

The Fateful Finger

Are sore fingers an occupational hazard for a quilter? How can there be joy in pricking our fingers over and over until they resemble chopped liver? There are all sorts of gadgets designed to save our fingers that can be found in quilt shops or advertised in the pages of our favorite magazines. To save my finger, I've tried little spoons and odd-shaped thimbles for the left hand and little tins of soft, sweet salve. I've looked at dimpled paddles and metal shields. I've felt the tips of needles to determine, like Goldilocks, if they are too sharp, too dull, or just right. Still I come back to the same old prick, prick, prick. Do you need, like I do, to feel the needle thrusting through the fabric so that you can poke it back in neat little stitches? I see people who sit at their hoops and frames, fingers iron-clad, needles darting, faces smiling. It is obvious that others can make those gadgets work. Anonymous quilters out there are saving their fingertips. They are making quilts with pristine, unspotted backs.

My problem is not a lack of enthusiasm for quilting notions. I am an adventurous person, and I would love to line up all the dollars I've spent to prevent digital mutilation. I'd have enough to finance the making of a king-sized quilt.

I guess I'm one of those people who need to feel that needle tip, who get a certain amount of pleasure from handling it as it skips across the quilt.

I've been working on a quilt now, and I've become obsessive about finishing it. It's a good-sized piece, and I've been getting up early, before first light, warming my mind with a cup of coffee and sitting down to quilt as the dawn colors the sky. I have worked for a month, from early each morning until after the rest of the world has turned in for the night. Then, in the quiet night, I fill the kitchen sink with hot water and gentle suds, and I wash the piled-up dishes. It feels healing on my battered finger. Quite honestly, it looks dreadful. But it gives me bragging rights about how hard I am working, and I do love the feel of the quilt working in my fingers. I am nearly done with my quilt. Only a little of the border is left to stitch. My finger is so battered that I would have to stop soon, anyway.

Now, I'll go off to guild meeting and show everyone my fingertip. I'll be delighted when everyone sympathizes. There is a sort of sainthood in suffering for your quilts. I will sit there in that guild meeting with my pricked finger and a halo around my head, and then go home and plan my next quilt.

Tripping Was Quite Fantastic

I've been on a quilt tour. All my friends have gone on tours. I have been careful to avoid them because I am New England thrifty, and I am quite aware of the financial temptations that are part and parcel of tour itineraries. The plans for this tour were so tempting that I will admit that I could not resist. I will say with pride, too, that despite my fall from fiscal grace, I came away from this one in better shape than most.

We prepared to board the bus early Saturday morning while the grass was still wet with dew and the rest of the world was still in bed. We stowed our suitcases in the compartment in the underside of the big, shiny bus and settled ourselves into soft, comfortable seats. I sat next to a window so that I could prop my head when I snoozed.

Promptly at 6:30 A.M. we pulled away from the parkside where we had assembled and headed west. As the sun rose higher and the sky turned bluer, we rolled past meadows with black and white cows chewing lush grass. We dipped down into a river gorge, shot up the side of the far bluff and on through a scene of patchwork fields and quilted towns.

At 11 A.M. we opened our sack lunches and by noon we had pulled up at our first stop—a bakery. Oh, yield not to temptation! Everyone piled off. I had protected myself by bringing only a limited amount of impulse cash in my purse. Everyone else bought sacks of cookies, lovely breads, and feather-light rolls. I was very good, except that, on second thought, I couldn't say "no" to a magnificent apricot pie, all golden and sugary. (Buying a juicy pie is not a very smart thing to do when one still has thirty-six hours of rough and tumble bus riding ahead of her. Nevertheless, I would carry it about with loving tenderness for the next three days and give it the scrupulous care required for a precious bundle.)

Next stop, next temptation—a quilt shop. I have never before seen an entire busload of women go bonkers at the same time. Once the bus door opened, the women burst from its confines like the seeds of a Touch-Me-Not flower being thrown upon the winds. They raced up and down the aisles of the shop, fingering bolts of fabric and feasting on the colors as if they were afraid that they would miss something wonderful (which they would not) or they were afraid there wouldn't be enough time (which there would be) or they were afraid that someone else might buy all the fabric (which no one could possibly do).

Then the pace slackened as they began to make considered judgments. They pulled out bolts. They pulled out more bolts. They piled up bolts, as many as they could carry. They stood in long lines at the cutting counters propping their loads on all available shelves and projections. Waiting in line in a quilt shop with one hand free is not a prudent thing to do. All about them hung scissors and templates and markers. On top of their bolts they piled their extra pickings. When their fabric had been cut and folded and stacked, each discovered that someone else had lovely fabric that she had somehow overlooked and back into the line they went. I have never seen such buying hysteria, all bottled into one place—forty-five quilters in heaven.

Back on the bus, my wallet was considerably slimmer. I had lost as much of my self-control as the other forty-four women. I arranged my paper bags and dutifully wrote my name on mine to identify each from my seatmates' bags and the bags across the aisle and down the aisle. Bags were being stuffed beneath the bus and under the seats. The luggage racks were becoming fuller in inverse proportion to the thinning of our wallets.

For three days we gorged on quilts. We talked quilts, looked at quilts, felt quilts. We listened to quilt stories, and we counted our quilt purchases as our bus trundled up and down back roads and through wooded lanes. We faced Temptations Four and Five and Six; and we bought and bought. We simply went berserk. When the cash ran out, we used our credit cards. It was lovely.

Of course, our trip was not spent totally on financial indulgences. I will remember always the sweetness of the quilters I met in their homes and around their quilt frames. I will cherish the friendships I made and the moments of laughter. I will savor the memory of the flavors and the fragrances on tables laden with sweet and spicy morsels of good "home cooking."

The last stop on the last day was a return trip to the big quilt store. The women tumbled off the bus, afraid that they had missed something on the first stop, hoping they would find one more wonder. I stayed in my seat. I had decided that I would not go in to surrender to one more temptation. I would behave myself, at least this one time, but a delegation of women came out of the store and clamored beneath my window to come in and see a new, beautiful quilt, and of course I went. I bought a set of expensive plastic templates. What's more, I would have bought the companion set if it had been there. I might never have a chance at finding them again. I wasn't sorry. I will not apologize to anyone.

The evening of that last day came, and we rolled across the dark countryside in our bus, through the night toward home. The lights of small towns winked through the windows of the bus in a friendly way. At midnight, the doors opened to spill out all of us and all of our bags with our names scrawled across them and all of our treasures tucked into our purses and pockets, treasures more precious than anything that pirates ever packed into trunks and buried in their caves.

Tonight will be a quiet time here at home. Tonight will be a time for accounting. Tonight, I will open my bags and lay out my treasures and count my baubles and recount my memories, and then I shall eat a last piece of apricot pie.

– – – –

Hair (Spray) Today, Clean Tomorrow

I have a social handicap that makes life difficult for me when I move among the Quilt Set. In my time, I have stood around a lot of tea tables at quilt show openings, I have sat at dinner tables with countless gracious guild members, I have helped myself to wonderful food around scores of potluck tables at guild meetings, and I have turned the spigots of a multitude of coffee pots set out at committee meetings. Because of my handicap, I have a definite feeling of social inferiority, a strong sense of societal ineptness. My problem is awkward to discuss, but being the good friends that you and I are, it makes it a little easier to say my problem out loud: I have, you see, a Leaky Lip.

There is something strange about the construction of my mouth. I don't know if my problem is the result of limp lower facial muscles or if the corners of my mouth turn down. Maybe it's because cups aren't designed to fit my mouth or because I love my coffee so much that I tend to chug-a-lug it, which is, in itself, not a particularly acceptable form of behavior.

I have learned to camouflage my inappropriate conduct. At a quilting bee, I never, never lean over the quilt frame when I am drinking coffee. At a fancy quilter's party, I try to be delicate about my behavior and hold a little paper tea napkin (usually printed with a dusty pink quilt block) up under my chin. At guild meetings I dab my napkin gracefully at my mouth and try to pretend that I am not a peasant.

I never spill on others, and when I stand while I am holding my cup I tend to lean slightly forward so that my coffee spills on the floor—though I have known the feel of warm drops splashing down the front of my dress.

What's to come of this? It's unthinkable that I give up coffee. I refuse to stay home and hide in my house where nobody can see me dribbling. I suppose that what's left for me is to carry on with my life as I have, to go on making my quilts, keeping them spotless by drinking my coffee in the kitchen and staying away from the snack tables at quilting parties. I will go on smiling joyfully at other quilters who are gracefully balancing their coffee cups on immaculate saucers and I will pretend that there is nothing wrong with me—that I, too, am competent in the beverage department.

Then, when I go home. . . . All honor to the pioneer who first conceived the notion that hair spray would remove ugly, accidental marks! God bless the quilter who was so imaginative that she first sprayed a ballpoint-ink mark on her quilt with hair spray. She saved me. Who'd have thought it? Hair spray will keep me clean and socially acceptable. Hair spray will eradicate my coffee spots and nobody, not anybody at all, except you and me, needs to know that the blot on my clothes was ever there. Now, there will never ever be a blot upon my quilt or a blot upon my name.

It's a Jungle Out There

It happened to me again. I can't believe I'm such a patsy. I was standing in the photo store going over some negatives with the salesperson. As I was about to order my reprints, I glanced up to see an anxious customer standing behind me.

"He seems to be in a hurry," I said to the sales clerk, "Why don't you help him. I'll wait,"

The anxious man had an order to place, He had, in fact, a lot of orders to place. The conversation went on and on, shuffling through papers, checking dates and information, laying out negatives, and squinting into the sun. I waited, and I waited.

"Surely," I thought, "He was in such a hurry, he will rush out at any minute, and I can get back to my business."

More shuffling! More squinting! More feverish conversation! I waited. I shifted my position against the counter. I waited.

Finally the man concluded his order, and I signaled the clerk that I would like to get on with my own business with him. He blinked. Then he remembered that I had been standing patiently all that time. I asked him to print several pictures before the evening closing time.

"Oh!" he said, "We can't possibly do that. That last order was a rush, and we have to get that one done."

Bill, my husband, had been waiting in the car. As I opened the door to get in, he asked what had kept me for an eternity.

"You remember the grocery store story, don't you?" I asked.

He remembered it well, the afternoon I had stood in a

long line with only six items in my arms. The woman directly behind me carried only a single carton of milk.

"Why don't you go ahead of me?" I asked.

"How nice of you," she replied, and then turned and called to her husband who was just emerging from a far aisle with a grocery cart piled high with cans and packages.

I had no clever retort on that occasion, either. I simply stood aside and let them pile $125 worth of groceries on the counter to be checked through ahead of me.

Whatever is the matter with me? Am I simply so stunned by such behavior in the market place that I am willing to be trod upon? Such thoughtless conduct is primitive and churlish. Obviously, as I stood meekly by, my mind was thinking up all sorts of snappy comebacks for these offenders. I am not at my best in a world where polite conversation might well be limited to, "You Tarzan. Me Jane."

That's the way the world is. I think it is a jungle, which is why I like to seek a haven in quilt stores. Quilt stores are different. The people in them are tolerant and caring. I can go into a quilt store, feel fabric, wrestle down bolts and spread them out across counters and tables. I can take all the time I want and chat with other quilters at the same time. They are gracious. They are kind. Nobody hurries me, and when I finally make my choices and stand in line to have my fabric cut and packaged, it is all done in a gentle, conversational manner, rather like a party, after all. These quilters are intelligent people who care. They are perceptive. They are courteous. They are civilized.

- - - -

I went to a sale in a quilt store the other day. Picture a sale in any other store, anywhere out there in the cold world. In other stores, people jostle, paw, snag, and clump. At the sale in the quilt store, every inch was filled with customers. They stood shoulder to shoulder, hip to hip, reaching over and under for bolts of fabric just beyond reach. They waited in long lines to have their yardages cut and bagged. A few husbands stood mashed firmly against the walls, somewhat bewildered but patient. There was laughter.

You hear of crowds reverting to animal behavior at soccer games and civil rights parades. You have certainly seen barbarous behavior on rush-hour buses and in freeway traffic. Every night on the television news we see loutish conduct on the international scene.

I have a great idea. What do you suppose would happen if international negotiations were held in quilt stores, if the peace talk delegates had seats between the red and lavender shelves, tucked in beside the soft browns. What if jury deliberations on difficult cases were conducted amid an array of new prints and stripes. There's a reason that fabrics are called "soft goods." I do believe they soften the spirit.

While the people in the rest of the world out there are swinging from vines and beating their chests, we quilters will go on fingering our fabrics and being soft-spoken, amiable, gracious, and obliging. Quilting is a civilized art, and we are civilized people.

How You Play the Game

Whoever it was who thought up that old saying about it not mattering if you win or lose could not have been a real person. It does matter! Every night I watch the sports coverage at the end of our TV news program. It always shows the winners, and the winners are always delirious with happiness. The professional baseball players pour champagne or beer or soda pop over each other's heads, The football players leap up high into the air and do dance steps over the goal line. The cheerleaders jump about waving their pompoms and hugging. Winning is pretty darn good. They rarely show the losers unless their coach has just been fired.

My three teenaged granddaughters are all high school athletes. They work hard at what they do, and they care about it a lot. They enjoy a challenge and winning is pretty wonderful. Losing is no fun at all, but they have learned to be gracious losers. Maybe their rivals were better. Maybe the circumstances were not good, like a player on their team getting hurt or a referee looking in the wrong direction when a penalty should have been called. Sometimes they just have a bad day. No, losing is not fun, but when you look at it, you can see that only one side, or person, wins. There are far more who don't win. That's what competition is all about and why people sometimes win and sometimes don't.

There is a direct parallel here to quilting, and it is not one bit far-fetched. Many of us enter quilt competitions. Sometimes it is at the county or state fair, sometimes at one of the big national or international quilt contests. When I enter one, I always send a quilt that is wonderful, at least in my own eyes. You and I have never made a quilt that wasn't invested with many hours of work and loving care. When we made it, we thought it was the best quilt we had ever sewn, maybe the best one that anybody, anywhere, anytime had ever sewn. Every quilt in any contest is made by someone who thinks exactly the same thing.

Every quilt is sent off by a proud maker, and only one will he a blue-ribbon winner, Only three quilts among them will receive any special recognition at all, and the rest of the beautiful quilts will hang unrewarded.

Like you, when I win a ribbon, I am ecstatic. It's a rare and glorious experience. When I lose, which is a great deal more often, I am disappointed. It's not a little disappointment, it's a big one, but I know when I send in my quilt that it will be shown in the midst of all those exceptional quilts. As sage Harry Truman said, "If you can't stand the heat, get out of the kitchen." If I can't stand the heat from the judges, I'd better keep my quilts at home and let my family tell me how good they are. My family may be prejudiced, but they are also gentle.

Of course, I am disappointed when I see that my quilt hasn't taken a prize, I smile a big fake smile just to let you know that not winning really doesn't matter that much, even though it does. Then, I make it a point to say nice things to those who do win. They have earned all of the delirious joy that goes with getting a ribbon.

The important thing is that the next thing I do is to read my critique. At this point, I get smart and pay attention. It's gratifying to know from the positive comments that the judges have found something especially good about my quilt. That part comforts my vanity. Giving some thought to the constructive comments is more important, however. Sometimes I realize that I can still fix a problem area. If the judge indicates that there is a knot on the surface, I can catch it with the tip of a needle and pull it inside. If the glare of the fluorescent lights has illuminated pencil markings I have overlooked, I can still remove the smudges.

I can add quilting. I can even rebind the quilt, if that is my problem. Major design changes aren't possible, of course, but frequently small improvements can make a world of difference. Then, I file the suggestions away in my head to be used for my next quilt, because I learn something new every time.

I know I sound like Pollyanna, but it makes sense to me to learn from my mistakes and maybe not make them again. I realize, when I walk through a quilt show and I am dazzled by the quilts that won and the wonderful ones that didn't, that every lovingly made quilt in that show is there because the quiltmaker is proud of her work. Winning is wonderful. Losing can be pretty good, too. That's how the game is played.

Special Delivery

My mailperson rang my doorbell this morning. She was a pretty young woman with short, sandy-red hair and slate blue shorts. A big leather pouch hung from her shoulder. As I signed the receipt for my registered letter, she shifted her weight from one foot to the other.

"May I ask?" she said. "Are you a quilter?"

"Of course!" I said. "Are you?"

You know she was! She's been delivering my mail for months, all those quilting accessory catalogs, advertisements from quilt stores, newsletters from quilt guilds, and that flock of other pieces of correspondence that you and I get.

I've met quilters in lots of unlikely places. I have sat across from them at potluck dinners. I have shared seats with them in airport waiting rooms. I have stood behind them in theater lines. One day, the checkout girl at the grocery store noticed the magazine I was buying and asked me if I was a quilter. I've always been amazed that, though we think of ourselves as a relatively small portion of the population, there always seems to be a quilter somewhere, everywhere. I did not, however, expect to discover that the person who delivers my mail is a quilter, too.

She had, she said, been initiated into the world of quilting at an adult education class. In the class, she had made twelve sampler blocks in six weeks. That alone is something of an achievement, two blocks a week. In the intervening two years since her class, she had walked around her assembled quilt top, studying it, not knowing quite how to go about quilting it. She had made excuses to herself, finding other things that she felt needed doing instead. Like all of us are wont to do, she put it off.

Finally, she sat herself down and explored this next step which was the quilting. She discovered two things. First, that it wasn't as hard as she expected and second, that she got better and better as she went along. Now that her quilting is finished, her sampler needs to be bound off.

There is always a spark of excitement when quilters discover each other, so you know exactly what happened on my doorstep. I dragged my quilts out onto the steps so that we could look at the bindings, and we did what quilters always do. We talked.

When she left, she did a quick-step. She was, after all, a working woman on her "appointed rounds," and I had delayed her. I could sense her excitement. That quilt of hers will get bound off, and, best of all, she has discovered that beyond every quilt is the next one.

I watched my mailperson striding across the lawns with her heavy pouch swinging from her shoulder. It brought to mind the motto inscribed on the Post Office building in New York City. The ancient quote reads, "Neither snow, nor rain, nor heat, nor gloom of night stays these couriers from the swift completion of their appointed rounds." I had the distinct feeling, as I watched her stride up the street, that she had discovered that mail delivering and quilting have much in common.

Nothing stops us from quilting, not rain nor snow nor heat, not gloom of night nor power failure, not running out of thread, not cutting the last piece of fabric wrong nor clock hands that move too fast. My mail lady is endowed with those resolute qualities that will not allow any obstacle, not natural disaster nor social commitment, to interfere with life's really important activities, like delivering the mail, and especially quilting.

- - - -

The Heiress

It was an astonishing phone call. She asked me, "Do you know anyone who could use some fabric? I'm culling my stash."

I was not generous. I didn't offer to share the fabric with a nursing home, or with a quilt guild, or even with my closest friends. Instead, I asked quite unashamedly, "Can I have it?"

This wonderful woman was a stranger. She arrived at my door, deposited four enormous, heavy trash bags on the floor of my workroom, and went away, just as mysteriously as she had come. Life was hectic at that moment, and I left the unopened bags lined up against my couch so that I could unpack them when I came home from a vacation trip.

I came home yesterday, and when I had completed the homecoming ceremonies (hot shower taken/refrigerator filled/washing machine started/mail sorted). I sat down to see what goodies were in my gift bags. On top was a large piece of brown velvet, just the right size for a jumper for a granddaughter. Underneath the velvet, calicos peeked out.

The more fabric I unpacked, the more delirious I got. The excitement was like being at a party, as I spread the rainbow out before me. I opened more bags and smoothed and folded and sorted and stacked. There were solids running up and down the scale, blending nicely into full chords. There were prints—flowery ones, blotchy ones, and geometrics. There were Christmas prints and Halloween prints, summery lines, and icy white-on-whites. There was a batik (a real one) and mini-dots and paisleys and plaids.

I began to separate the fabrics into piles. Then I resorted them according styles, and then according to colors, and then into sub-groups of tints and shades.

Please understand, I am not a lady who is without fabric. I have two closets full of fabric, floor to ceiling, and my arrangement for storing that material is not ideal. Once, long ago, all of my fabrics were arranged neatly, cut into useful shapes and trimmed free of schnibbles. They were smoothed and folded into uniform packets and stored in bins. Each bin was clearly marked by color. These bins were stacked in my two closets, one on top of another, and they looked very neat. If I had left my fabrics stored in that manner, they would still be neat. However, I use my fabric.

To get at the fabric that is stored in this way, I stand on a good solid chair. Not a folding chair, because they tend to buckle and grab my legs and try to break them. It is also not a good idea to stand on the top step of the small kitchen ladder, the step that has a stenciled sign on it that reads, "Do not stand on this step." I stand on an ordinary kitchen chair and wrestle down my bins. In the process, all of the bits and pieces of fabric that have been stuffed into the crevices around the bins tumble out. Threads and snippets dribble over the sides. Usually, the bin I want is the one on the bottom of the pile.

Everyone has a dream. My husband, Bill, has a dream. He deals with our dreams, his and mine, by buying one sweepstakes ticket each week. Then we sit and sort out our plans for what we will do when we win the big prize. The first thing on the list for Bill is a new computer. The absolutely first thing I am going to do is to have a new workroom with an easy-to-see, easy-to-get-at fabric storage arrangement. Like the famous Little Dutch Boy who put his finger in the dike, if I don't find a way to control this fabric flood, I'm going to drown.

My dream room will have a shelf around the perimeter about 22″ high. On this shelf will be bins, clear plastic ones of a manageable size. The bins will sit side by side, never piled on top of each other, so that I can see all of my fabric. They will be big enough and plentiful enough that I can store my material without packing it in so tightly that it is crushed and impossible to see. Underneath, on the floor, will be another row of bins for the dross of the same color, those little pieces that are full of holes and have rough shapes, but are just too good to throw away because, someday, I might need a little triangle just that size and color. When I am ready to make a quilt, I will simply take off the lids of my bins and sift through my rainbow.

Now, I have these four huge new piles of fabric, folded, sorted, and piled on the floor against my workroom couch. I haven't sat on the couch in years, because of the surplus fabric I have piled on it. There must be some place where I can put this new material so that it is available. It should be visible. It should be up off the floor, because I need that space to prepare my new quilt for the frame.

Many years ago, there was a TV show called "The Million-aire." It was about a generous rich man who, each week, hired an attorney to find somebody and give that person a million dollars. My mysterious friend gave me a "million dollars" worth of fabric. The fact is that this material needs to be stored in such a way that I can find it and use it. Where? How?

There are several options. Of course, moving to a bigger and roomier house is not one of them. I could make the piles on the couch higher, or I could move the couch to the base-ment and replace it with shelves to hold my treasure. I could store some of it in the spare bedroom. I could sew it into new quilts, though somehow, when I sew, the size of my pile of fabric never seems to dwindle. It only grows.

Being an heiress is a glorious thing. It has its rights and its responsibilities. My right is to enjoy this fabric, to use it, to cut it, shape it, and stitch it into wonderful pictures. It is my right to make quilts, soft, luxurious, colorful quilts with it, and right now, my responsibility is to find some place to put it.

A Message from Mother Goose

A quilt block came to me in the mail. The nice lady who sent it said she couldn't make her points come together and would I help her? It was a funny block. The lady was right. The points didn't come together by two inches, I'm not kidding. She wanted to make the block right so that she could make a whole quilt, and the vision of a whole quilt with blocks that don't meet by two inches was very funny indeed, or so I thought.

I bought myself two dresses, jumpers that slip over my head and fall comfortably loose, almost to the ankles. I loved those dresses. They were made in blue plaids, and when I wore them, I felt unencumbered and casual. The only problem with those dresses was that they were not what the designers call high style. That means, in merchandising language, that they had no pockets.

I need pockets. I tote tissues and pencils in my pockets, things that I find indispensable. Like Lucy Locket, I had no pocket. "Well," I thought, "that's easy to fix. I'll just open up the side seams and put in a quick pocket on each dress."

Yesterday morning, I got out my seam ripper, and I picked out serger threads on both dresses. I opened up a six-inch area on the right side of each dress. With a paper pattern that I had made from a pocket of one of my other dresses, I cut pocket pieces from dark-blue fabric from my stash.

I worked on the first dress all morning, trying to insert the pocket. I've made dresses in the past, sewing one pocket piece onto the front side and one onto the back side of the skirt, and then sewing the whole skirt together, whipping down the seam from the waist, around the pocket, and on down to the hem with my zippy sewing machine. I discovered yesterday that putting a pocket into an already-finished dress is not that easy.

First of all, there's all that ripping and pulling out the snippets of polyester thread that cling to your fingers and clothes. That is followed by fitting the edges of the pocket pieces in place to the front and the back of the skirt. Every time I sewed down one piece, I caught the other side of the skirt into the stitching by mistake. Over and over, I ripped out my seam and began again.

By noon I had the first pocket inserted perfectly . . . upside down. It was not funny. I thought about the quilting lady with her red and white block with points that didn't meet by two inches. I wondered how many times she had sewn that block together, how many hours, how many wrinkles in her forehead, how many tears she had shed. Her star block was not funny.

I've made lots of quilt blocks. Some have gone together perfectly. Some have taken a bit of maneuvering to work around the minor glitches, like sewing the quilt block to the leg of my jeans or snipping a hole where no hole was intended to be. Usually, the block works out well with only a bit of fussing and a dab of patience. Pockets shouldn't be that much different.

I removed my upside-down pocket, and with careful attention, I sewed it in right side up. Since I had already opened up the side of the second dress, I wrestled the second pocket into place, sewing, snipping, and resewing to get it right.

Last night, as I took two aspirin with my cup of coffee, I thought about the lady and her block and me and my dresses. Maybe the lady makes lovely dresses with ease, adding flounces or pockets perfectly and in jig time. Maybe that is what she does well. Setting in pockets is not one of my talents.

I wrote the quilt lady a long letter. I made some suggestions about how she could make her points come together. I redrafted her pattern. I signed the letter, sealed it, stamped it, and walked to the mail box. As I opened up the slot of the corner mailbox, I sent her a mental message, a sort of blessing. I hope that her piecing problems evaporate and that she makes her new blocks perfectly and effortlessly. May they go together easily and sweetly. Though she struggles with quilt blocks and I struggle with pockets, like the butcher, the baker, and the candlestick maker, she and I are both together in the same tub, rub-a-dub-dub.

- - - -

A Workshop Is a Trying Experience

Whenever an exciting quilting teacher comes to town and I feel the need for inspiration, I sign up for a class. Let me tell you here and now, that in a workshop, I am an unequivocal dud. I find the lighting unrelenting, the lack of my favorite tools frustrating, the cacophony of other students around me distracting, and the forced creativity painful. Everyone else seems to throw herself into the learning challenge with boundless energy, but not me.

I took a class last fall from a talented, famous teacher. The object of the workshop was to create a color "experience" using a single, repetitive, simple shape cut from an enormous variety of tints and shades and textures. The teacher was really good. As he spoke, he spread out an enormous trove of colored stationery, construction paper, wallpaper, transparent colored film, and metallics on the classroom tables and invited us to help ourselves, to immerse ourselves in the excitement and emotion of color.

The room was filled with creative and clever people. They seemed to know exactly where they were going and what they were doing. Even one small, nine-year-old boy snipped and glued with enthusiasm. Excitement permeated everything as collages began to grow and spread across the walls.

Let me tell you how I coped—I hid. In the classroom was a closet with a sink in it that was meant as a place for making coffee. It was quiet and isolated. I staked out my "claim" in

- - - -

that closet. I sorted colored shapes on the drainboard of the sink. I cut and glued my paper quilt, tearing off scraps that "felt" wrong, re-cutting, re-gluing, and re-working. I struggled, finding myself near tears of frustration. I wrestled with making my colors blend together, my pieces fit and match. Outside my closet, the delirium went on.

The teacher found me. He brought me out and set me to work in the middle of all those high achievers. He thought that I should work in better light and a freer atmosphere. The tiny closet had been my refuge. My struggle was an embarrassment.

At the end of the day, we studied our paper quilts as they hung on the walls, and we talked about them. Some of the other collages were quite wonderful. My own quilt was mediocre, but acceptable. Oh, how I had wanted to do something spectacular!

We swept the cut-aways into the trash bin and picked up our tools. The teacher neatened up his spectrum of delicious colors for another day and another class. We went out into the icy twilight. I passed a flower bed of white roses that were frozen into a delicate blush by the early freeze. They were crowned with tufts of new white snow and backed with the deep, rich green of evergreen shrubs pocketed with snowy mounds. I was suddenly overwhelmed with the richness, the subtleties of the hues and tints.

I drove out of the parking ramp and stopped at the traffic light at the corner. How many times have I looked at traffic lights and never realized that the lens of the light is covered with a hexagon grid? I had never noticed the array of red or green shadings that shine from the tiny honeycomb shapes. As I drove east toward the river in the darkening city I glanced up and gasped. I saw that the setting sun behind me had turned the windows at the top of the high buildings a fluorescent, astonishing, hot, hot pink.

I realized my workshop expectations were wrong. The mediocre paper quilt I produced was not important. Instead, the creative struggle that had gone on in my brain had produced a new awareness of color. It made me open and vulnerable. It introduced me to astonishing and novel trains of thought. The workshop, in reality, was not meant to help me construct a paper quilt to take home and hang on my wall, but it forced me to open my mind to possibilities that I had not even known existed. The creativity it demanded was painful, and definitely not easy, but the class was meant to exercise my senses, to push them further with new challenges.

I will take another workshop before long, and I am sure that I will be a dud again. When I go home, I may have a clumsy, ill-conceived project in my sewing case, but, lucky me, my head will be bursting with the undreamed riches of possibility.

Tell-Tales

Do you know the old saying that goes like this: "You can tell a person by his or her clothes"? It has a great deal of truth in it.

Recently, I was at an art show where there were displays of stunning, hand-crafted clothing. Some had pieced trimmings. Some were painted and dyed. Some had insets and appliqués. Some had arty cowl or scarf necklines and smooth, fitted seams. I spent a good deal of time watching people try on these garments, posing in front of mirrors, turning this way and that. They were clever, attractive people, making choices of complementing colors and lines that emphasized their best features. Watching them admire those things told me something about them. It told me that they were discriminating people who appreciate craftsmanship and fine design.

I watched the shoes walking by me and wondered what they told me about their wearers. There were dainty fitted slippers, army boots, jogging shoes, and shoes with tiny spike heels. I myself was wearing sensible, ugly oxfords perfect for standing on a concrete floor. That tells people that I value my comfort.

Many men who came to that show wore hand-painted ties, glorious big silk ones. Those men love strong color and startling designs. I marveled at them, since I am married to a man who believes that, "It isn't a tie unless it is striped." I felt the urge to buy a bold, daring tie for Bill, but I knew that if I did, it would be left hanging in the back of our closet, where it wouldn't tell anyone anything.

Some people wear quilted vests studded with pins from around the world. Those people, it would seem, are travelers. Dramatic clothing tells me that the wearer is, herself, dramatic. Someone who wears a garment with simple lines that looks as if it were molded for her body alone, is very sophisticated.

Sometimes, clothing colors are soft. Gentle grays and lavenders are worn by people who appear to be subdued and controlled. Bright colors are worn by people who want to make a loud, clear statement. Sometimes, very neat people wear white. These people do not tend to spill coffee down their fronts.

When I was in the office services store the other day, a stunning woman walked in. She wore a perfectly fitted black suit, black stockings, and black shoes. On her head was a tailored black hat, and her makeup was meticulously, artfully applied. She walked past me to the counter, and as she stood with her back to me, I saw that her skirt was covered with cat hairs. That lady is, of course, a cat lover.

Last night, Bill and I went to a dinner meeting together, where he had to make a speech. As he rose and walked past me on the way to the podium, I saw that he had a long, white basting thread dangling from the back of his suit jacket. It is not unusual for me to have threads on my own clothes. What did that thread tell the world about him? I refrained from reaching up and snatching it as he walked by. That basting thread should be worn with pride. It is a badge or a Medal of Honor—an ornament of distinction. It identifies our area of endeavor and achievement. A long, white basting thread, worn with panache, says, "Here, World, for all to see, is a quilter . . . or a quilter's spouse."

Chapter 4

------- A STITCH IN TIME

Time Flies When You're Having Fun

Standing at the cashier in Montgomery Wards is not my idea of a good time. You can stand there a long time while the girl behind the cash register explores the inside seams of garments for price tags. She riffles through old receipts, rustles tissue paper, and shuffles decks of credit cards. All the while you wait, you peer over the shoulder of the lady in line in front of you, who has a lady in front of her. I waited there last night in the harsh glare of fluorescent lights. The mirrored wall behind the cashier threw back a reflection that was so dismal it was worthy of being emblazoned on any passport. I studied myself in the hard, gray light and realized with a shock that indelible tire-tread marks scaled the sides of my face, up the edges of my eyes, and across my forehead. In that strange illumination I looked as though I had been knocked down at the Grand Prix, and the entire cavalcade of racing cars had driven across my face. When I had plunked down my dollar and a quarter for a genuine imitation leather address book, I fled the store to a climate of softer, more generous lighting. What I had seen, I told myself, was a sort of Dorian Gray picture. Surely, time had actually stood still for my body. I am, after all these years, a young woman. I still feel thin and agile. I work hard. I have lots of enthusiasm. The apparition in the mirror must have been a prediction of what is still to come.

Now, I wonder, who am I kidding? Do I really believe that I have been living a life of eternal youth? The wrinkles are already here. I ask myself, what has happened to me in these years since I received my first copy of *Quilter's Newsletter Magazine*?

Well, I've made a lot of quilts. I hope each one has been better than the previous one. In these years I have learned to make smaller stitches. I've learned to draft more accurately, to use adventurous colors. I remember being told that one should never put orange and red and pink together. Well, I like red and orange and pink, and now I have the courage to use them together—the oranger the better. I have learned to make quilts that please me.

I have created a place for myself. In this room, I have moved all of the books out of the tall bookcase and replaced them with quilt books. I have moved the TV into the living room and closed the door. The "family room" is now secure, and it is mine. In these years, I have found a place of my own, where I can mess and create, I can think and stitch. I have quiet and solitude or a gathering place. In these years my friends and family have come to tolerate, and even appreciate, my need for a time and place of my very own.

Life has changed for all of us. When I began to try to remember what our world was like way back then, I was astonished. This is what it was like in the Dark Ages:

There was not a single quilt store in this city. I kept a list of all of the places where a few bolts of cotton fabric could be found. It included basements of drugstores and dark back corners of fabric stores that displayed great front shelves of new polyester blends and cushiony double-knits. There were five-and-dimes with hard, glossy 36″-wide percales for 59¢ a yard. The colors were limited, and when the textile industry finally understood that there were quilters "out there" who were looking for cotton fabric, they produced a supply of tiny-print calicoes with the harsh mineral colors of the 1880s. We all knew every fabric design on the market and combed our stores for anything new. We bought quarter-yard pieces of everything and piled them in rainbows on the shelves of our closets.

Now, the choice of fabric is overwhelming, and the displays in the huge fabric stores blind me. I frequent the small quilt shops where it is easier for me to find the bright, bold colors of the spectrum sliding down a whole series of softer choices. "Way back then" I hung a quilt show for one of the local colleges. Those prairie quilts were lavender and spring green and yellow. Now we can choose from half a dozen shades of purple, and the greens range from olive through a breathless, misty aqua.

Back then, the available batts were mostly fluffy piles of polyester that had to be patted into place, the holes filled and smoothed. Cotton batting was available from the mail-order houses, but it had to be stitched closely to secure it. It had nothing to bind it together. We cajoled and begged our fabric stores to stock a batting that was glazed and controlled. Back then, nobody had ever heard of fiber migration.

– – – –

Some of the quilt batts had patterns on the paper wrappers, and if we were lucky, they had packages of quilting needles included. The needles were always number sevens. Then the stores expanded their supplies and stocked number eights. It was some years before they discovered that people were interested in nines and tens.

The thread of the '60s was cotton. It made a pearly white stitch that showed like tiny beads on the surface of our quilts. Then the thread industry produced a "better" quilting thread of polyester. There are lots of people now who like it, but I'm timid about it because it feels like wire to me and I have visions of cutting my quilt. I'm glad the thread people are giving us a choice, now. I've noticed both kinds of threads on the store racks this past year.

Years ago there had not been a quilting symposium, no conference that gathered people together to share ideas, history, patterns and the excitement of new discoveries. Earlier, except when a few major spectacles were staged by the batting manufacturers, quilt shows were mostly confined to small groups, many in churches, who displayed quilts by folding them over the backs of chairs or hanging them from clotheslines. The shows were attended by the curious and the quilters' families. Think about the quilt shows now. Shows now are hung with imagination and viewed by crowds. They are staffed by volunteers of all ages—young women with babies tucked beneath the admission tables, husbands hauling armfuls of plastic-wrapped quilts, medium-aged people with cameras, and those super-mature people like me inhaling all of the excitement. Quilt shows are vital places to be.

Quilt clubs were small organizations, sometimes six or seven people gathered around a frame. Quilters still gather around frames, but now the network of these groups stretches across this country and across the world. And the most wonderful part of this phenomenon is that we have found those quilt groups on the next street and across town. Big guilds have grown from this, as gathering places to share and re-charge on a regular basis.

Those years ago, quilting was learned from grandmothers or neighbors. Nowadays, the menu of classes offered in shops and schools is awesome. Years ago I could count on my fingers the quilt books that were available. Today we can spend precious hours in quilt stores browsing the many racks of books.

When *QNM* was born, it was a slim black-and-white publication. It was a tender thread to the anonymous quilters somewhere else. Look what's happened to it! It grew and blossomed into color. It grew new leaves. It dropped its seeds, and new magazines sprang up. Now, a variety of glossy, good magazines are slipped into our mailboxes monthly.

We have been freed from the economic necessity to produce warmth for our family, from the compulsion to use up every scrap of fabric. We can go to the store without guilt and buy glorious fabric. We can stitch a bed cover; we can stitch a picture; we can stitch clothing. We can play with geometrics. We are encouraged to be creative. With all of the long line of wonderful traditions behind us, supporting us, we can take off—we can fly.

When I first began thinking back to my life all those years ago, I thought, "There's not much difference. I'm still making quilts." I've lived long enough that it doesn't seem so long ago. Then, I mentally put myself in this same chair in this same room years ago. I pictured myself planning a quilt, and I could not believe what Time has done for us. We have become a community. We share with and support each other. We belong.

Twinkle, Twinkle, Feathered Star

P*reface to the drama*: My dear friend, Jean, came into my home carrying the box reverently. She placed it on my lap and said breathlessly, "Look what I found in my mother's attic." Inside were bits of fabric, curled, folded, and creased. There were shades of orange and yellow and some white. There, too, were several short lengths of these same solid-colored fabrics and a number of pieced Feathered Star blocks.

"I counted them," she said, "and I'm sure there are enough blocks that you could make a quilt of them for me." Her excitement was like the electricity in the clothes dryer.

"Yes," I said, "someday when I have the time I'll see what I can do."

I put the box on my work table. Since then I have carefully walked around it. I have piled books on top of it. I have shoved it back behind my table and buried it with quilts.

Time: One year later when I have reached the limit of my quilt-quota.

Scene: A warm, quiet summer afternoon in my workroom.

Characters: As for the characters, I was to be astonished how many there would be in this story.

I enter. Carefully I lift out hundreds of pieces of fabric and begin piling them about me on the floor. I sort and press and tie them together with threads. Identifying the diamond and triangle scraps consumes an entire day. In the early coolness next morning I begin to examine the pieced blocks. I lay them out side by side, and as they lie there on my carpet, I begin to hear a story. The Feathered Star quilt squares are talking to me. The story is mostly about nameless women, but their imprint on the things I find in the box is undeniable.

When I have sorted each scrap and square, I discover five complete 14½" stars. They are well pieced. The center point, at which all the little triangles come together accurately, is properly swirled to flare the seams evenly. A sixth block lacks a diamond on an outer point. The box is filled with scrubby fabric tidbits obviously kept in case any single piece needed extending, but there is not a thread of the star-tip color. Did that first quilter run out of fabric in the color for the outer points? Did she abandon the project to the attic because she could not find a color to match?

Quilter Number Two discovered the box in the attic. In it, she found the original templates, cut precisely from an old Kodak box. With new material she carefully cut out more squares, thinking that she could match those first blocks and stitch enough to fill out a quilt top. It would appear that the Feathered Star design was beyond her skills. She stitched four more blocks and put the project back into the attic.

Enter Quilter Number Three. She discovered the box with

all those quilt blocks. Perhaps they were musty, even dusty. With plans to use them, she washed them. The thread shrank. It puckered. It pulled into hard little knots. The back seams wavered and raveled. They were out of control. Back to the attic went the box.

Quilter Number Four entered. She discovered the box. It now contained two sets of blocks, the templates, and the extra material. This quilter sat herself down to piece. She was as excited as I would have been. She plunged headlong into her work and did not stop to study the templates. She laid them down on the fabric, traced around them, and cut them out. She had pieced together four blocks before she understood that the templates were intended to have the seam allowance *added*. They are astonishing blocks. They are not neat and smooth. They are small. Somehow, however, she managed to sew the pieces together and when she realized what she had done, discouraged, she put those four blocks into the box and left them in the attic.

I am Quilter Number Five. I am overwhelmed by the job I have committed myself to do, but my determination is a thing to be reckoned with. The first six blocks come out of the box. I snip puckered threads and work with an iron to carefully manipulate each block until it lies flat. I appliqué the edges of the folds into place and eventually each block is smooth and square. From the newer material in the box I cut one extra star tip and stitch it into place—an evil-eye patch. The additional blocks are unusable, but these six blocks are rescued. I set them with alternate blocks cut from the 36″-wide white percale in the box. The short lengths of orange and yellow are cut into strips. I play puzzle games on the floor with them, arranging them in patterns to create a border. I mark the blocks for quilting, a dahlia pattern with a starry center.

Quilter Number Six will quilt the top into a family treasure.

I do not think this is an unusual story. Instead, I think it is the story of many quilts. The hands of six quilters will have made their contributions over a span of half a century. The quilt will chronicle a series of generations. It is a diary. Born in the Depression years, these stars have hung on the horizon for fifty years. They now shine full and bright. Well, bless my lucky stars! Mellow and glowing, they 're right for wishing.

Happy Days

M y husband and I have spent days in the midst of the whirring, grinding machines at the library media lab transferring all of our old family movies to video tape so that our kids can absorb the family history in a convenient way. Night after night we have threaded fifty-year-old films onto large reels and watched the images flutter across the TV screen. Sometimes the brittle film cracked. Sometimes the torn sprockets slipped and the pictures clattered past our eyes. The old black-and-white film has remained sharp and clear. The early colored film has turned sepia. Generation by generation, we have filed the family onto the video tape and witnessed some momentous times in history. There are pictures of an autogyro, of the carving of Mt. Rushmore, of the incompleted span of the George Washington Bridge thrusting out above the Hudson River. There, too, are Bobby Jones playing at the Augusta Golf Club and Bill Tilden swinging his famous tennis racket.

Last night we had our film premiere. The children and their families gathered in front of the TV, bags of popcorn strategically placed. It was a wonderful first-night crowd, dressed magnificently for the occasion in faded jeans. The atmosphere was electric.

Then came the exciting moment. The house lights dimmed. Children nudged each other in the ribs to pay attention. Parents hushed each other. So began our family history on the television screen.

I sat entranced by the excitement of seeing my grandfather who died when I was four years old. My husband laughed at my antics as I kissed a chubby, cherub toddler. Then, I became aware of an interesting fact. It was this: Each of us, as we sat watching, was seeing something different.

"Hey, Mom! Are those penny loafers?" asked a grown-up child.

"Look at the bobby socks!" exclaimed another.

A ten-year-old granddaughter thought the Lindy Hop was "cool," but the waltz, where we touched each other, was pretty hysterical.

For myself, I could feel the excitement as I whizzed down the hill on my sled and exploded over the ice bump at the bottom. I could smell the salt spray in the air as it billowed through the boat sails.

I thought about my life then and about my life today. I suddenly realized there were no quilts in the movies. No quilts! How could anything that means so much to me today, that absorbs so much of my time, have been totally absent from my childhood? No quilts!

I searched back among the memories of growing up, of marrying, of raising five children. I remembered the same things everyone does: the childhood holidays, the adolescent inadequacies, the excitement of the first job, the sleeplessness of being a new mother, the frustrations of tracing the activities of growing children, and finally the birth of the grandchildren. There it was: my life. But where were the quilts in those movies?

Somewhere there is a single snapshot of me as a tiny baby lying in the altogether on a quilt. I know now that it was my mother's wedding quilt. She didn't make it. It was a gift. I remembered as a child that I used to trace those rose patterns with my finger in wonderment. It covered the big four-poster in the guest room. That was the only quilt in my past, and it wasn't in those movies.

My love affair with that quilt must have been pretty strong because there was no question in my mind that when I married, I, too, had to have a quilt. I remember asking my mother how to make one, and she admitted that she really had no idea. She had never seen a quilt made, but "forty years or so ago" she had stashed away an old quilt kit that she had fallen heir to, and the pieces were in a drawer "somewhere up-stairs."

By golly, as mothers are wont to do, she found it. From that moment, I was on my own. The Rose quilt was a bit faded at this point. I studied it, stitch by stitch. The needlework was flawless, minutely buttonholed with pearly floss to out-line the wreaths. I was lucky to have this "teacher" to set high standards for me at the outset.

For two years I appliquéd and embroidered. When I was married in 1948, I had my first quilt. During the following years my life was over-filled. It always was. It still is. And yet, quilts kept happening. I suppose that it was not until 1970 when I found other quilters that I was able to share my ob-session, and quilts stopped being an invisible part of my life.

Last week I sat at the hospital as one of my children mended from a broken hip. I stitched on a quilt square, and as I worked there in that room, nurses brushed by me and commented, "I have a quilt at home," or "My grandmother made quilts," or "I'm so excited. I'm taking a quilting class, and it's wonderful."

What's more, other people began stopping in to see what I was doing: the head nurse, the woman from the room next door. A doctor commented, "Hey, I like that."

Quilts may not show in those old family movies, but they were there, just as surely as I am sitting here today. They were in my head and in my heart. The only difference is that those of us who loved them then are able to show the rest of the world about quilts now. Have you noticed that they have become a universal language? Some people are quite proficient at *it*. Some are only just getting the hang of *it*, but people are getting to understand *it* better and better. If I were to make a movie now, there would be quilts in it, lots of them. This is a good time now when quilts have become part and parcel of our everyday lives—a universal joy.

New and Improved

I don't think I am an old fogy! I appreciate all the new things that have been invented, the telephone, the self-defrosting refrigerator, and the rotary cutter. I enjoy shopping for new fashions in the store, and even if my age prohibits me from wearing miniskirts, I admire shapely young women in theirs.

Then, I wonder, why am I fighting change? It seems that lately everything is being tampered with. My shampoo has been "new and improved." The old shampoo used to clean my hair and leave it shiny and shaped. The improved version of the same shampoo makes my hair limp and drab.

I live in fear that someone will meddle with camera design, and my fifteen-year-old camera will become obsolete. I have finally learned how to make it behave and do the photographic tricks I need it to do. If they improve it, I will not be able to get my same old films, batteries, and equipment that I have become used to, and I will have to begin all over again, learning from ground zero.

Every time I go to the local fabric store, there seems to be a new "ester" on display. Man-made polyester fabrics may be great for wash-and-wear clothes, but when we try to piece those fabrics into our quilts, they shimmy and slip.

"New" used to mean a new concept, something never done before that would make our lives fuller and more meaningful. Now "new" is a marketing ploy that may change our favorite products next year, next month, or next week.

Even though advertisers may think the buying public is addicted to "new," sometimes "old" is just fine. One of the cola companies quickly discovered that if you monkey with something good, the public protests loudly. They came to understand that the concept of "classic" is not only acceptable, it is cherished.

I've been making quilted wall hangings lately—small, manageable pieces that are currently very much in style. I've been playing with all those new fabrics in the quilt stores that are printed in marvelous patterns and colors, and I've been experimenting with the new tools. I've tried making attractive contemporary clothing, too, skirts in long, flowing lengths and nippy little vests. I've been very "now" and "new."

"Classic," though, has always been an accepted concept for quilters. I've noticed that at every quilt show, the raffle quilt (or opportunity quilt, or whatever) is an old-fashioned, full-sized quilt to cover a big bed. The pattern running across the top may be made in those bright contemporary fabrics, but the old idea of a quilt covering a bed is still the traditional sentiment.

We make a quilt to cover a special new baby. For an intimate wedding gift, we make a bed quilt. To make a guest room especially welcoming, we put a quilt on the bed. The time-honored idea is that a quilt is to be slept under because it is a comfort.

We are quiltmakers because we love the feel of fabric and because we enjoy the satisfaction of shaping it into clever patterns, but quilt lovers also seem to have a basic instinct. We have a need to provide security and warmth. We need quilts on our beds.

A bed quilt may have been made with a "new" polyester batt and the fabric colored with "improved" dyes. It may have been cut with "high tech" tools and stitched on a "computer age" sewing machine. That quilt may be the result of "state-of-the-art" technology, but the "old-fashioned" feelings of caring and sharing and generosity are still the quilt's basic ingredients, all stitched together into a blend of comfort.

Just Keep A 'Rollin', Wagon Wheels

A friend asked me, not long ago, if I have a computer.

"Yes," I told her. "I use it to write. I happen to be the World's Worst Typist, second only to being the World's Worst Hand Writer. My computer lets me write easily and corrects my mistakes without scrubbing eraser holes in my paper. Why do you ask?"

"Everybody says I should get one."

"Do you want one?" I asked her.

"No."

"Then, why in heaven's name should you get one?"

It seems that her family and friends have been pushing her to buy a computer because they think she should use it to design her quilts.

The magazine ads for quilt-design programs are enticing and the demonstrations at quilt affairs are intriguing. Colors and shapes twist and whirl and dance on the computer screens. Many people have gone mad over computer-generated quilt-making. For them, computer designing has been liberating and challenging. It has made it possible for them to conceptualize their quilts quickly and easily.

I spent an evening with another one of my friends. She was playing with her computer quilt program, making the blocks do flip-flops and handstands. She was frustrated, though, because she couldn't get the kind of star she wanted to display on her screen. It seemed impossible for her to conjure up the particular diamond shape she needed.

She worked feverishly, poking and prodding her computer keys. She made jiggly, clicking noises and touched her EN-TER key. Lights flashed, things moved and danced and spun. She perspired. She poked more keys. She perspired some more. She simply could not manipulate it to give her what she needed.

I said, "Here. Give me a pencil." I drafted the star and sent her to the copy store to print it a few times. We laid the copies out on the floor and played with the big, full-sized patterns. I, myself, function better with a concrete approach, touching and manipulating my designs rather than working with abstract ideas traced out on a screen. I enjoy the activity and the feel of working directly with my fabric and patterns. Some people do.

When my husband, the computer man, heard about our design session, he said, "Helen, you're a wagon-wheel maker." He waited long enough for me to wonder what obscure point he was trying to make.

"When the automobile came along, all the old wagon-wheel makers were left sitting out in the field watching the sunset."

Bill is one of those people who like to see patterns gyrate across a computer screen. He enjoys moving and altering shadowy electronic ideas. All I need from my computer is the ability to type out words quickly and neatly. One night while I was quilting in my workroom, Bill passed me, headed for my desk. He had a look of anticipation, as if he were itching to make my computer do something new and exciting. I astonished myself. I roared at him, "Don't touch my computer."

Every time I have turned on my machine to write a letter, I have found new things leering at me from the screen, clever surprises like personalized messages and handy-jim-dandy new charts and tables. As I said before, some people like to play with computers.

Bill is right. I am a wagon-wheel maker. I love to tinker with my hands. I like to pinch and pin and whittle and scribble, clip and stitch and dabble. That, for me, is part of the fun of quiltmaking. Though computers are liberators for some people, others find satisfaction in the challenge of tinkering and shaping and assembling.

A case in point: When my antique cuckoo clock died, I took it from one clock store to another. The clock repairmen only knew how to insert new batteries or chips or other space-age gimcracks. I finally found an older man who unscrewed the back of my cuckoo clock and went deep inside the chains and wheels and put it in order.

When he returned it to me, he had lovingly oiled the carved pheasants on the front so that their dyed feathers gleamed against the ancient wood. He was a craftsman of the old school who found a deep satisfaction in the gentle touch of his materials. We understood each other.

So, all of you out there on the road, roaring off to someplace in your glorious, computerized limousines, wave as you go by. I'll be sitting out in my field, leaning against my wagon wheel, watching the sunset.

That's About the Size of It

A quilt 72″ x 90″ seems like a good size to cover a dormitory bed. My granddaughter is going away to school and she has asked me for a special present. She wants squares from the fabrics left over from my quilts. She wants to sew them together to make a comforter to take away with her. Then, she will be able to look at the fabrics in this new "quilt" of hers and be reminded of my bleeding heart quilt and my marigold quilt and my morning-glory quilt. She would like to make my leftovers into a flower garden of her own.

I went to the quilt shop this morning. The shop was ringed with batts arranged neatly all around the tops of the fabric shelves. There must have been fifty to seventy-five of them. "I want a 72″ x 90″ batt, for my granddaughter," I said, "comforter thick."

The shop owner said she didn't think there was such a thing. "Then," I said, "I'll take two of regular weight, and I'll double them." She hunted through her supply.

"None," she said. "In fact; nobody uses that size anymore."

I leaned against the counter and thought about the state of the world. People are changing. Beds are changing. Quilts are changing. I realize, now, that this change has been happening quite clearly, and I had hardly noticed it. For instance, there is a little boy who lives behind us. On pleasant evenings he bounces his basketball against his garage. The little boy is now, suddenly, taller than his father. I notice, too, that another of my granddaughters has grown long and lean. She looks like one of those gorgeous, leggy fashion models. People are growing big. So are beds.

Last week I invited a friend up to see a quilt I have hanging on the wall above my bed. My bed is a double bed, and the quilt on it measures 82″ x 96″. My friend was surprised. She said, "Do you sleep in that little thing?"

I told her that I have been sleeping in "that little thing" for many years. Later in the week, a friend whom Bill and I were visiting found it necessary to apologize to me that her bed was "only" a double bed.

Beds from the past have had a variety of measurements, mostly small. I was astonished when I first saw the Norwegian beds in the old peasant cottages. Apparently, people in old Norway slept sitting up. They may have done this so that they could sleep with their heads elevated or, perhaps, to make it easier for the man of the house to leap up and protect his family in the night. The beds were amazingly short. Small covers would have fit them quite nicely.

Old Dutch cupboard beds were short, too, built high into the wall so that any flood that might come would wash beneath. The space inside was so cramped that the sleeper slept curled up. She pulled herself upright with a rope that was hung inside. Bedding for those beds could not have been very large, either.

In the 1970s, I had my first experience with changing bed sizes. My daughter, Connie, wanted to make a quilt for her

- - - -

boyfriend. He had, she said, a king-size bed. I bought a king-size batt (120˝ x 120˝) and drafted a pattern to cover it. There were to be twenty-four blocks and a large border. Connie began piecing all those blocks. It seemed that it was going to take forever to make this really big quilt. She was well along in the process of cut-pin–stitch–press, and we were laughing and talking together one lazy late autumn afternoon when Connie happened to mention that this quilt was to cover a waterbed! What size is a waterbed? How do you cover it? We made a trip to the waterbed store to investigate. We discovered that though waterbeds are enormous, a quilt should fit neatly only the top of the bed, and not hang all the way down to the floor. We eliminated the border, and the quilt fit perfectly.

Back in the Dark Ages when I began making quilts, beds came only in baby, twin, and double-bed sizes. Queen size, king size, waterbed size, and all sizes in between had not even been invented.

Now we need to buy my granddaughter a king-size batt and teach her how to cut, chop, pare, and fuse it all back together again and make it just the right size. That, in itself, might be a skill worth cultivating. It would seem that to make quilts, nowadays, ones that actually go on beds, ones that we can tuck about us and sleep under contentedly, we need to be flexible. We have a lot of options. A word to the wise: mind the size.

And I Will Make Thee Beds of Roses

I have four daughters. They are Muffin, Jojo, Connie, and Faithie. Those are not their official names, the ones listed on their birth certificates. Those are my names, given to them when they were tiny, and though these children of mine are now grown, mature women living in a society of sophisticated adults who call them by their formal names, they still tolerate and even cherish my use of these affectionate ones. These names are personal. They represent my love. So it is with quilt names.

I saw a lovely quilt the other day. A young woman, named Sarah, glowed as she spread it out reverently before me. She explained that this was a quilt her grandmother (also named Sarah) had made out of clothing scraps. The quilt, she explained, was called Sarah's Aprons. I knew the pattern was called Dresden Plate. That was the name in all of the books. Everybody knows that. Certainly, Sarah must know that her grandmother's quilt was a Dresden Plate.

I'm glad I had the good sense to hide my thoughts. It was obvious to me later, when I thought about that quilt, that since Sarah's grandmother had made it, her grandmother herself must have known what the pattern name was in all the books, but she had conceived that quilt, made it, and named it Sarah's Aprons, and therefore, that was indeed its name. We can identify its Dresden Plate design from the pattern book, but the essence of the quilt will always be her grandmother's.

When you look through the quilt pattern books, you see the names of people who might have slipped into anonymity but for the affectionate names given to their favorite quilt patterns. There is Aunt Sukey's Choice, Peggy Anne's Special, Pharlemia's Favorite, and Anna's Pride. There, too, is the Carpenter, Shoemaker, Bachelor, and Old Maid who inspired puzzle blocks. These designs bear the imprint of the people who made them.

Sometimes, too, our own quilt blocks are named for a place, an event, or something fond and familiar. We make quilts with abstract patterns, triangles and diamonds and squares spinning across them, and somehow, when they are done, we find we need, as with our children, to name them. We give them names that tell stories, indicate our relationship to them, and then we go to show-and-tell and we hold our quilts up and tell all the world about them.

Most of my quilts have old block designs that have relevance to the meanings of the quilts. I feel an interconnectedness with early quiltmakers. I empathize with the women who first stitched the old blocks and named them for the things they loved. I take those quilt blocks and make them into my own, dubbing them with my own pet names. Early quiltmakers must have felt awe when they saw a Storm at Sea quilt. When I see a Storm at Sea, my childhood comes back to me, and I picture myself standing on the shore of Chesapeake Bay and watching the winds blow and waves churn and swell. The pristine Pine Tree block evokes memories of ranks of evergreens marching up the sides of New England mountains. That Pine Tree block has become mine.

The astonishing array of quilted rose designs indicates special meanings to more people than any other flower blocks. Roses are sprinkled across quilt tops, twisted into graceful wreaths, sprawled on quilted vines, appliquéd, pieced, and stuffed. Rose patterns with a dozen or more names are imbued with special, cherished meanings, such as Rambling Rose, Rose of Sharon, Rose Basket, and Rose Dream. Every time a rose is chosen and stitched, it becomes a personal pattern. If we choose, we can call it by its name in the books, or we can give it our own name. We can call it Backyard Rose or Summer Rose or Early Rose. Whatever we call it, in essence it becomes My Rose.

Art and literature, too, are full of roses. Bobby Burns wrote, "My love is like a red, red rose," and Gertrude Stein said, "A rose is a rose is a rose," but Shakespeare said it best when he said, "A rose by any other name would smell as sweet."

Beautiful but Dumb

Long ago, when I was young, every girl's dream was to be popular with the boys and to have a date every Saturday night. We worked very hard to be beautiful. We studied the fashion magazines to learn how to dress cleverly, For this, we wore pleated skirts, soft sweaters, and little pearl necklaces. Saddle shoes and bobby socks were obligatory, and lucky was the girl who could sweet-talk her father into letting her cover it all with one of his big shirts with the tails hanging out.

According to the code, a young girl must never ever be smarter than the man she was dating. Even if she had the IQ of Marie Curie, she must never admit to it. Girls did not take math in school, I was one of only two girls in my geometry class. (Thank goodness for that geometry. I use it every day in my quilting.) Instead, girls took French, English literature, and cooking, which was intended to prepare them for their place in the world—that of delicate, fragile lady of the home.

That world was a million years ago, Now, the study of geometry, French, literature, and cooking holds bounties to be reaped by everyone, and what's more, the experts in these fields are bright people who are sought after and admired. Nowadays, smart is fashionable. Hooray!

However, I am a fence-sitter, the product of both ages, then and now. I still envy the beautiful people, and I still find myself trying to decide if wisdom is cleverness or if cleverness is sometimes not very bright.

- - - -

Case in point: I have been helping a group of talented needlewomen put together a quilted wall-hanging for their church office. I drew the image of their church building set on a squashed central diamond that pokes out to narrow points at the sides, The women have appliquéd and pieced the center diamond precisely. Now, it is my responsibility to set that diamond shape, all pointy and devious, into the quilt. I have fudged, smoothed, creased, ironed, and appliquéd to make those points sharp, straight, and perfect. As I worked, I wondered to myself why I drew the pattern this way. Wouldn't it have been much easier to have set that church picture in a square on point? Was that elongated diamond with the devilish side points beautiful, but dumb?

Why do obscure angles, difficult fabrics, and perfect curves lure me? Do I find a kind of masochistic delight in struggling with them, or is the ultimate pleasure in my triumph over them? I think this compulsion that I have is to make something a bit different, unique. Sometimes, the difference is so minor that the quilt may look only imperceptibly nicer, and then I discover in the making that it takes an extra week's worth of picking, poking, pulling, and prying to make it work. Certainly, making a quilt like this is doing things the hard way.

When I analyze my planning process, it seems that there is no dazzling clarity to my logic. I have a vision in my mind. In it, my quilt has pieces here and there that are a bit out of the ordinary, small variations to add a touch of flavoring, a bit of excitement, a freshness. I know that these differences will require extra hours of work, but at the time I am planning the quilt, I don't care. Instead, I simply plunge in, cutting, piecing, and wrestling my way through these devious angles and junctions. In the effort, I prick my fingers, and the wrinkle between my eyebrows gets deeper.

Making a quilt is always more of an effort than I had planned, unrealistic as I am. I am a dud when it comes to efficiency expertise. The "easy way" is simply not in my vocabulary. Nevertheless, I am an old-fashioned girl, and I may be dumb, but I love a beautiful quilt!

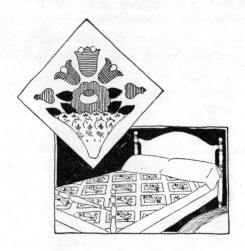

Stitchosaurus

I am a dinosaur, and I know it. What's more, I am happy to be a dinosaur. It's what I was meant to be. I am a hand quilter. Normally, I am not a patient person. Standing in line at the grocery store is one of my least favorite things to do. Having a telephone operator put me on hold, waiting in the doctor's office, or standing at a bus stop is less than satisfying for me. A late mailperson sets me pacing on my doorstep.

Hand quilting requires a lot of patience, so if I am an impatient person, why do I hand quilt? Let me tell you about the show I went to see. Nearly all the quilts were beautifully machine quilted, each requiring that the quilter have stamina, energy to control a quilt as it is fed through the machine, and dexterity to manipulate it into flattering stitched shapes without pleats, puckers, or stress lines. These quilts were creative. They were stunning.

Then I came home and sat down at my quilt frame once more, to stitch and stitch and stitch by hand, pricking my fingers and picking out unsatisfactory stitches, restitching here and there, then standing up to stretch my stiff muscles and have a cup of coffee. I understand full well why people work at their sewing machines to get their quilts sculpted and fluffed quickly, so why do I, an impatient person, keep coming back to my quilt frame to hand quilt my work?

I'll tell you why! This morning, as I sit here at my frame, the sun is coming up outside my window in a rose-colored sky. Clear lamplight spills across my quilt. Music plays on the radio behind me, I am quilting the background of this picture of a Welsh church with a towering steeple, set upon a fabric printed with rolling green tree tops. As I work, stitch by stitch, the trees tell me how to quilt them so that they will spring to life. My mind plays fanciful games, and I breathe dimension into this quilt. As my eye moves across the quilt, inch by inch, I find the tiny imperfections, a thread or a knot, the little things that happen when I make my quilts. These tough spots are easy to put to rights. A machine would have galloped over them and never have discovered them. I watch, to my delight, as a quilting line etches depth; the scene is becoming a reality.

As I work quietly, my thoughts wind here and there, experimenting and solving and delighting me. This is my kind of meditation. I am not sure if my hand quilting is any better or any worse than the glorious machine quilting that I saw yesterday. I know that the thought processes and the work discipline are very different. I first began quilting because I liked the feel of fabric and the deftness of the manipulation. I like this feel of new creation. When I machine quilt, I sew something that is attractive and appropriate and a hundred times more expedient, but it makes me tense. When I sit here and hand quilt, I feel a sort of jubilation. I feel quieted.

I've been working on this quilt day and night. There comes a time in the life of every quilt, whether machine- or handmade, that the quilter says, "Enough is enough." Today, I shall put in the last quilting stitch and finish it. Thus, another era in this dinosaur's life will be history.

– – – –

Our State Fair Is a Great State Fair

This morning I feel as if a marimba player has been beating on the calves of my legs with shiny, spangled mallets. This is The Day After.

Yesterday, Bill and I got up in the cool of the early morning and went off to the fairgrounds before eight. Even at that early hour, hundreds of people were milling about, buying tickets, and lining up. Music blared from the loudspeakers, and the morning dew evaporated in the sun.

Tradition says that we must be there early to wait with the crowd of people gathering outside the Creative Activities Building. We bought hot coffee in paper cups to sustain ourselves during the hour that we stood there and talked to strangers. Strangers became friends.

At nine, the great doors were rolled up, and the crowd crushed inside. The quilts were displayed in wonderful profusion, mingled with the embroidery and hooked rugs and stamp collections.

One historian describes the first Minnesota State Fair in 1854 as a small affair held in a single building with three rooms. The first floor was used to display corn, pumpkins, and beans, but on the second floor, fifty or more women gathered to watch in amazement as a man demonstrated a new machine that actually sewed fabric. Since that groundbreaking event, the State Fair has been an arena for new and wondrous things, giant harvesters, prefabricated farm buildings, and snowmobiles. The same charged atmosphere of 1854 has repeated itself all across the years.

As recently as thirty-five years ago, the quilts on display at the fairgrounds were mostly soft pastel Dresden Plates and Grandmother's Flower Gardens. They were pieced neatly and quilted with commercial patterns that you could buy for a few cents at the needlework counter in the local Five-and-Ten-Cent Stores. Those quilts were sweet and predictable. The quilts I saw yesterday were far beyond predictable; they staggered my imagination. There were watercolor quilts and origami quilts, quilts made with hand-dyed fabrics, and quilts made with batiks and Caribbean prints. There were quilts done in minute, perfect appliqué, and piecing done in dizzying geometrics. In the excitement, people crowded in and pressed their noses against the glass cases to see the intricate quilting more clearly.

During the rest of the morning, Bill and I roamed other parts of the fairgrounds and listened to the hawkers peddle their wares. We watched bungee jumping and displays of fish and beavers and deer at the Natural Resources Building. At noon, of course, we ate deep-fried veggies followed by a giant piece of strawberry shortcake.

Thus well fed, we went back to the Creative Activities Building, to see which of our quilter's guild friends were sitting in the booth demonstrating their stitching on their latest projects. The crowds thronged through the building and milled around the special case where the sweepstakes winners were hung in their pristine glory.

In the afternoon, we listened to a Dixieland band, a French café accordion band, and a Medicine Show band. We wandered back to watch the crowds explore the quilts.

The afternoon lengthened into twilight, and we stood along the parade route to see the lovely llamas with their soulful eyes. Enormous horses hitched together pulled a monstrous red beer wagon. We ate ears of buttered corn. By eight o'clock, fatigue was beginning to set in. We made one more trip back to the Creative Activities Building to be sure that we hadn't missed anything.

As we were leaving, in the glow at the end of the day, fireworks whistled and blazed in a dazzling display of color, bursting against the sky like a great, exploding quilt.

This morning I am weary. I have a sunburned nose, my legs feel bruised, there are strawberry stains on my shirt, but I have been to the fair. I have made my annual pilgrimage. I have walked with thousands to the sounds of laughter and the blare of music, and I have seen the quilts. Now that I have come away and I am home, I have marked my calendar carefully. It says, "Same time, next year."

Chapter 5

THE TIES THAT BIND

Kissin' Kin

I come from a family of remarkable women. There's Cousin Julie the photographer, and Sister Nancy, the flower expert. I have a daughter who makes computers do acrobatics, and one who knows all about the best sort of recreational equipment. One daughter can make large kitchens function flawlessly and one is a minister's wife, which is a profession all its own. I'm glad that, in this clan, my claim is to be Helen, the quilter.

When we gather for family get-togethers, we women stand in the living room and talk at each other. The men go outdoors.

When I say talk "at" each other, I want you to understand that we talk at the same time, but no one misses a beat of the conversation. There is a sort of family electricity that flows among us and we hear every word that the others are saying. I listen in astonishment to the wisdom and exploits of these amazing women, and at the same time I know that I, myself, can talk freely, volubly, and sometimes with a bit of exaggeration, and that I am never, ever in danger of boring the others. You see, we like each other.

I listen at these gatherings to the pleasures of Japanese flower arranging and whether a fiberglass or aluminum canoe is best. We all unanimously admire the small children who have escaped to the playroom or are eating the salted nuts. The atmosphere is exciting. It's an opportunity. It is prime time for quilt talk, and with my sermonizing I am creating quilt converts.

All of these women, every single one of them, has learned how to make blocks for friendship quilts. Julie, the photographer, has finished a quilt for her daughter's wedding and, success having gone to her head, she is planning a second one for her son's anniversary, She is obviously a daring woman. Ingred, the computer programmer, is assembling a quilt for a friend who is moving away, and she is stitching together childish, crayoned quilt squares for her church. She is a lovely daughter. She listens to her mother. Connie, the kitchen wizard, has made five quilts now. The others, too, have all become quilt-types.

At our gatherings now, we arrive with soft bundles tucked under our arms and we lay out quilt squares on the carpet. We discuss design and color. We talk simultaneously and enthusiastically about quilts. The men still go out into the yard.

Up by the Hair on
His Chinny-Chin-Chin

I have a dilemma: "dill" as in pickle, "lemma" as in lemon. I created it all myself. In the first years of our marriage, we wore out my mother's wedding quilt first and then my own wedding quilt. The poor beauties were drab and tattered along the edges from being sat upon when we put on our socks. The quilting stitches were snapped from yanking the covers up under our chins to keep warm during the cold winter nights. The fabric was battered from persistent washing. Those poor quilts were utterly exhausted.

Some fifteen years ago, I sewed one of those cross-stitch quilts that come in kits. It was attractive, friendly, and I made it to be slept under. The backing was brushed flannel to keep it from sliding off the bed, and it was long enough to be tucked in at the bottom so that we did not wrestle it up and leave our bare ankles exposed. With a minimal amount of creative thought and a maximum of fabric and batting, it was a perfect sleep-under quilt.

When I took it off the bed this spring, it was worn across the top. The edge was raveled, the fabric weary and soiled. Into the washing machine it went. The soil came out. I re-bound the edge and darned the thin, broken areas. It was almost as good as new and certainly good enough for sleeping beneath.

My husband has gained an appreciation for quilts over the years. Perhaps "appreciation" is not an adequate word. Perhaps I should call it "respect," or perhaps "awe." He looked at the damage on that quilt with horror. He sighed a gentle sigh and mumbled something about wanting to keep warm up under his chin. He is a tall man. I assured him that I had made the quilt for sleeping under. Some quilts are made for that— for warmth and contentment.

I woke up the other morning and discovered him asleep with the quilt turned carefully back and a towel swaddling his chest and neck. I was horrified. I pleaded with him to roll up in the quilt. I offered to sew an old-fashioned chin-wiper across the top of it to protect it. "No," he said sadly. He was wearing it out.

I have spent a day on the dining room floor, wrestling with twelve yards of innocuous calico. I made a huge mattress-cover-type thing, stitched a piece of batting inside, and tied it all over with boring yarn. It was very hard to make this uninteresting "quilt." I had bought the calico when I was visiting a friend in Ohio. I had the impulse, as I worked, to at least piece a large Ohio Star into the top. Then I reminded myself that this thing that I was making must not have anything attractive about it or my husband would fold it carefully back under his arms, protecting it, and exposing himself to the chill of the night. I resisted creative temptation.

All day I sat tailor-style on the dining room floor running that enormous needle threaded with yarn up and down across the top, thinking all the time that it would have been so much more fun to machine quilt my dill-lemon. Up and down went the needle.

I have finished my husband's comforter. It is huge, long enough to tuck well under the mattress and to pull up high under his chin. It is soft and dollopy. It is dull, totally void of any creative effort. It is warm. We can batter it, yank it, scrub it, dub it. When it is worn out, we will throw it away. But for now, it will lie in all its dowdy softness underneath the gentle glory of a lovely pieced quilt that I use as a spread. There they are, the two of them: Beauty and the Beast.

I'm a Calculating Woman

My family is mathematically adept. At least, five of us are: one husband and four daughters. They do remarkable things with logarithms, calculators, and computer languages.

My own life has been spent feeling totally inept because I am a person who cries when I have to balance my checkbook.

Several years ago, my husband sent me to a Math Trauma clinic, and it did a great deal toward building my self-esteem. It taught me that it doesn't matter what method I use for my math so long as I get the right answer. Now, when I pose a math problem to my family they discuss it with impressive competence and lengthy digital manipulations on their calculators; they come up with the answer that I got in a few short moments by multiplying by ten, dividing by two, and adding three. My methods are very logical to me, but they confound everyone else. It is satisfying to know that I don't have to do it the way I was taught during those painful years of basic algebra. Though my family may be versed in Boolean Algebra and the Pythagorean Theorem, I do just fine with my own brand of Kellian Calculations.

Currently I am trying to formulate my quilt calculations, such as the Law of Probability: Given how many corners and how many seams, the chances are 99.99 percent that a seam of the bias binding will fall exactly at the place where you have to miter a corner.

- - - -

Also in the bias category comes this formulation: If you calculate the exact number of square inches of your fabric before you cut your continuous bias, you will always have either way too much or just a bit too little for your quilt.

Another point to ponder: Given the precision of our current cutting and sewing tools, a simple Flying Geese strip will always grow longer than it should be. Likewise, a large star will expand as it moves out from the center, getting wavier and wavier.

Conversely, with the same tools, any 12″ block that you piece will be ?″ to ¼″ smaller than required.

Here is another law to consider: When you miter a corner on your border, you can measure it with a protractor, mark it with a triangular template, fold it back at a 45-degree angle, and press it. You can trim it, pin it, and sew it, and in inverse proportion to your meticulous care, the corner will either bulge or get a pointed dog-ear.

One immutable rule I've made for myself when measuring or calculating is: I don't ever cut anything off until I am absolutely, positively sure it works. The creativity required for inserting corner blocks on too-short border strips, inserting triangles in mitered corners that don't fit together, and applying decorative piecing to inadequate backing boggles the mind.

Mathematically speaking, subtraction is always easier than addition. I haven't even begun to probe the implications of multiplication and division.

Over-Taxed

Right now we are celebrating The Annual Spring Rite of the Income Tax. My friends say, "Oh, we have an accountant," or "We do that January 1 and get it out of the way."

Not so at our house! About mid-March I feel panic begin to rise in my breast. I know what is ahead. I begin to nudge my husband, gently at first. I sympathize with him that he doesn't want to prepare the tax forms any more than I do, and it's his bad luck that he's capable of doing them. If I were to do the taxes, we would both sit in a federal penitentiary someplace and reflect on my fiscal inadequacy.

The mailman has brought the forms; our receipts are filed away in brown envelopes; the checkbook is balanced. You'd think the rest would be an easy task.

Bill has set me up at the little personal computer with my account books spread out in front of me. My own job should be simple. All I have to do is key into the computer all of my expenses with their identification. Last night while I sat in front of that little machine, I began to enumerate all those dollars that have flown through our bank account this past year. The house was totally quiet. I needed that. No radio, no talking. Bill leaned over my shoulder and watched.

"A quilt can't cost that much to make!" he said.

Little he knows! It takes a lot of thread, fabric, stencils, batting, pencils, paper, and magazines to make a quilt. You know what I mean—you make quilts, too. As I listed my fabric expense, I saw that it was humongous. I reminded myself that the several hundred dollars for fabric entered in my checkbook doesn't explain that some of the fabric I bought for a quilt didn't work, and I had to put it away. It doesn't explain that the fabric wasn't wasted because I can use it another day in another quilt. It doesn't explain, either, that one never buys the 2½ yards of fabric that one is going to need because one might cut it wrong, or it might shrink and one might need more; I usually buy double what I calculate. It also doesn't explain that sometimes one buys fabric that one doesn't specifically need, but it is so wonderful that one might need it some other time. It DOES explain, though, why my fabric cupboard is so full that I have begun to pile material on the couch.

Then there are other items—the sewing machine, which was a fair purchase. Bill acknowledges that, but with the machine came the purchase of accessories that were too delicious to ignore: a new light, a new chair that was just the right height, and, of course, all that fabric for experimental roughage.

Then I took pictures, and I took more pictures, and I had the pictures developed, and then I had additional pictures printed to send to all my friends.

The phone calls added up. I've made so many wonderful friends who live in faraway places, friends I've met at quilting conventions or sometimes even when I was sitting in a quiet place, quilting, and a perfect stranger came up and sat beside me to see what I was doing—only that perfect stranger is now a good friend at the other end of the telephone.

I went on keying in the check amounts and the explanations. There was a wonderful quilt I had bought. It needed to be bought!

Bill leaned over my shoulder and watched. He didn't say anything, but it made me uncomfortable.

All of this accounting was making me aware of my quilting extravagances. It was not, however, making me penitent. I will do it all again next year.

When we have the year's expenses adequately tabulated, my husband will take all the amounts like insurance payments and property taxes and food, and he will sit down with the dreary tax forms and fill them out. He will finish at eleven o'clock the night of April 15, and we will get into the car and drive to the post office. We do this every year. The ritual is a sort of celebration. All of the hundreds of other people who have put off calculating their taxes until the final hour will be in their cars lined up, all heading in the same direction. The lines will snake across both bridges and down Third Avenue. They will converge at the post office where the postal attendants will stand in the middle of the street with big mail sacks. We will drive by, throw in our IRS envelope with a shout of "Thank you," and "Have a good day," and then find ourselves a quiet all-night restaurant for a piece of pie, a cup of coffee, a quiet contemplation of next year's situation, and a promise that we won't do this last-minute tax thing again.

But we will.

- - - -

Celestial Navigation

I watched a movie on TV. The two stars had shining, beautiful faces. "Our marriage is so wonderful," she cooed. "We are perfect. We know exactly what each other is going to do and exactly how we think about things. We're so alike!"

Well, goodie for them! I am married to a man who is poles apart from me. If he is dealt a hand of bridge, he will study the entire hand (while the rest of us go crazy), and when he has decided every card he is going to play, he makes his move. He wins every time.

When I play a game, I want to get on with it. I am not trying to solve the riddle of the sphinx.

Some years ago, Bill and I hung a mobile together for a community affair. It was a painful experience for me. It involved long deliberation, careful measuring, deep thought, some eye-squinting, and thoughtful weighing and analysis. When the mobile was finally up, it was a piece of art. If I hadn't bitten my tongue but, instead, had impatiently taken over the project, I would have had it up in a matter of moments—lopsided. I'd have balanced it by taping paper clips here and there, or a drop of glue or a safety pin, until it straightened itself out. I'd have made-do, jerry-rigged it. Bill's job was perfect. I knew it would be. It took a lot of time.

Bill and I have learned a lot of tolerance, patience and admiration for each other over the years.

- - - -

The spectrum of quiltmakers must be like the two of us. I see some incredible quilts when I go to quilt shows. When I look at the big winners all beautifully colored and balanced and stitched—so perfectly—I wonder if the maker has ever had time to make another quilt. The degree of detailed perfection is so astonishing that I am sure the quiltmaker must be very old.

When I make a quilt, I leap into it with great enthusiasm. My favorite reply when someone asks me how I made a quilt is that I do a lot of ripping. I figure if I sew something on and it doesn't work, I can rip it off or appliqué over it. I'm not sloppy about what I do, I just can't wait to get started, to get up in the night because I can't wait to quilt, to jump out of bed in the morning because I am excited to discover if my colors are going to work, if my plans are going to fit, if it's going to look right, if it's going to do what I want it to do.

Usually it does, and if it doesn't, like I said before, I rip. Bill doesn't "rip" whatever he does. He doesn't need to rip anything, when he finally gets to doing whatever it is he is going to do. Two different modes. His surer, mine faster. Like navigators, we are those poles apart.

One of the reasons I am so anxious is that I always have another quilt in my head waiting to get out, and I need to finish "this one" so that I can get on to the "next one." I quilt and I pile up my quilts, quilt and pile.

I sat next to a lady once on an airplane. She asked me what

I like to do, and I explained to her that I was a quiltmaker. She was curious, amused, a bit credulous. "What do you do for your work?" she said.

"I quilt."

"What do you do in your spare time?"

"I quilt."

She couldn't quite grasp what every quiltmaker in the world would understand. Quite simply, it is this: that I quilt all the time. I do not agonize about my quilting. I do not analyze it. I do not weigh, squint, or sit for long hours calculating it. No, I pick up my scissors and fabric and I quilt.

"Oh," she said. "Then you must have a lot of quilts."

"Yes," I acknowledged.

"You must have so many. Do you sleep under them?"

"A couple."

"Where are the rest?"

"On shelves, stacked on beds, in piles on the floor."

"But what do you do with them all?"

"That's easy. I finger them. I feel them. I count them. I spread them out and look at them and love them."

The lady was astonished. I was a strange sort of person like she had never met before. I was a quilt lover, an impetuous quiltmaker, a quilt hoarder.

"How interesting," she murmured, somewhat skeptically.

"Yes," I said, "I am a quilt fanatic. I have lots of quilts. I am making one right now."

What's more, when this one is done, I am going to begin another one. I have a hint of color, an exciting idea glimmering on the edge of my mind. I have already begun to save fabric. It may or may not work. I'm not making a critical decision. Right now, it's "Hurry up and get this stitched. Bind off. Vacuum up the hodgepodge of threads on the floor. Leap into the next."

Bill admires my quilts. He sleeps under them. He enjoys them hanging on our walls. Sometimes he stands and studies them as I work. After a long period of patient musing, he will make a considered suggestion. I always listen. We work well together. I know he has thought things out carefully. He will be right. He's always right. He drives me crazy, but he's right. He's my rudder. When I'm quilting up a storm and lose my sense of direction, he keeps me headed right. We may be navigators who are poles apart in style, but when I'm making quilts, we chart a pretty snug course together, for better or worse.

Snips and Snails and Puppy Dog Tails

As you may know, I raised a whole flock of little girls. There were my four daughters, a series of foreign students, and my three granddaughters. I thought I knew a lot about children. Let me say right now, after a week of babysitting my grandsons, "Boys are different."

That's not to say that little girls are perfect. I still have the TV tray with the inky foot prints marching across it, stamped by some unidentified child. The girls tattered their clothes, and there were daily disputes. No, little girls are not perfect. What I discovered, after three days with these small boys, is that little boys throw things. They take things apart, they shout and make loud noises. They thrash about, rock violently in rocking chairs, and slam doors. The sheer energy that radiates from little boys is astonishing.

Don't misunderstand me, these little boys were good. Yes, they indulged in a fair amount of teasing, sibling rivalry, and strewing of cracker crumbs about the house, but I believe that they were quite normal. I can tell you now, however, that I have never ever seen such creative use of silverware, Tinkertoys, and rubber bands. Ballpoint pens became lethal weapons.

For my own protection, I wedged a large four-by-four styrofoam insulation board across the doorless opening to my workroom. My scissors, needles, rotary cutters, and yardsticks are a small, creative boy's dream. I took each boy into my room separately and explained to him "secretly" that I had put up the barrier to protect my quilting tools and that I knew that I could rely on him to be my special sentinel and watch to be sure that nothing would be touched. I was not so foolish as to believe that any mere, flimsy piece of styrofoam would keep out a curious, creative boy.

Each boy took his personal responsibility for the care of my things very seriously. My quilting tools went untouched. When the boys were watching *The Jungle Book* on TV, I slipped out to stitch a bit. My styrofoam-fenced work space was a sanctuary.

Their childish attention spans were short, and it took a good deal of spontaneity and creativity to keep ahead of them. Hearty and frequent applications of snacks and milk kept them preoccupied. Now and then, I soothed myself for a few moments with a needle in my hand, feeling fabric and stitching on my quilt. I am not used to hurled objects and explosive shouts. They were good boys. I'm just not used to boys.

Now, they have gone home. The house is quiet. I will replace the lamp chain that was mysteriously yanked out of its socket, and I will reset the station push-buttons on my radio. Sudden noises still startle me, but my pulse doesn't race quite as rapidly. I have swept up cookie crumbs, wiped off finger prints, and scooped up LEGO toys. Once again I can quilt in peace. I miss the boys.

– – – –

Ode to Joy

Christmas has always been a twelve-month season at our house. Anyone who understands why a person makes quilts instead of going out and buying a faster, cheaper blanket can understand why Christmas has become a way of life for some of us. The sheer joy of creating something, producing a gift from our own hearts and hands, takes over our lives.

Since I was a tiny child, I remember the prime directive was to give from the heart. I made calendars from stiff cardboard and old Christmas-card pictures as gifts for my aunts. For my uncles, I did creative things with packages of shoelaces. All year long, I worked at these gifts. They were stashed in hiding places in the backs of closets, in bottom drawers, and under beds. The Christmas morning excitement was almost unbearable as people opened my presents and exclaimed with delight.

By first grade, I had learned to sew, and I cross-stitched pot holders, the kind you could buy at the five-and-dime store, pre-padded and bound. The uncles got the obligatory calendars and shoelaces.

As I grew older, I embroidered dish towels and samplers. When I got to high school, I learned to knit. My uncles graduated from calendars and shoelaces to socks.

Then I bought a sewing machine. This was the turning point of my life. That machine introduced me to the cutting and shaping of fabric to make Christmas presents. Fabric was pleasant and soft. The precision of the sewing machine needle biting through fabric to create perfect lines of stitching was satisfying.

When I married and began to raise a family, I introduced my children to the joys of giving gifts from the heart. They, too, produced calendars and shoelace creations. They poked cloves into oranges to make pomanders, tucked lavender into net bags for sachets, and they, too, learned to sew. The children made pot holders and dish towels, and stashed them into their own hiding places, to be brought out and tucked under the tree late at night on December 24th. There came a time when I had grandchildren, who made their own versions of Christmas treasures.

Christmas is coming around again. What sorts of treasures am I planning? One of my best Christmases was the year I made wall quilts for them all. I called them A Few of My Favorite Things. My very favorite memory that I pieced and appliquéd was the one I made for my daughter, Faith. When she was four years old, she had made a gift for me—a framed piece of felt with a red stick Santa Claus wearing black boots and a tasseled hat, I quilted a replica of the stick Santa and surrounded it with tiny pieced pine trees. She didn't have to tell me how much my quilted memory meant to her. I knew.

This is the zenith of my life. Now that my children are busy inventing things for their children to make, I have time to sew something just for myself. I shall make treasures all year for ten months. I shall address my Christmas cards early and have my presents already stashed away for the giving time, because this year, I am going to give myself a Christmas present. Right after Thanksgiving dinner, I shall set up my quilt frame in the dining room, and for one month, I shall quilt on my new quilt. I will listen to carols on the radio, and I will stitch, while the rest of the city is rushing about in the snow and ice. I will thread my needle and pass it through the quilt, and feel the rush of pleasure it gives me. I will feel the peace of the season in the peace that quilting gives to my soul. I will savor my quilting, stitch by stitch, and moment by moment, and when Christmas Eve comes, my quilt will be finished. I will take down the frame and set the dining room table and feed hot rice pudding to all the family. We will put our treasures under the tree and be joyful.

When the Christmas holiday is over and we have taken the tree down and swept up the fallen needles and wrapped the decorations and put them away, it will be time to begin the ritual all over again. It will be time to let our love wonder and our imaginations wander over the possibilities of what we will create for next year. It will be time to begin stitching and stashing. I will have finished my new, soft Christmas-time quilt, and it will be time for me to nurture Christmas joy in my heart for another season.

To Dye, Perchance to Dream

I bought a piece of border fabric. It was a reproduction of an antique print. Rich red and blue flowers bloomed on a ground color of a gray-brown mushroom. When I tried to match the background to solid-colored fabrics in the shop, every gray material I held against it turned brown, and every brown cloth turned gray. On all those rows and rows of shelves, there wasn't a single credible selection. Even the unbleached muslin refused to blend successfully.

I came home and dug into my stash to see what I could find, but there was nothing compatible in my thirty-year-old collection.

"Well," I said to myself, "It's a grayed, drab, dirtyish sort of color. I'll just make some of it myself."

Since I needed the same sort of color that happens in the washing machine when I make a mistake and throw my black sweatshirt into the wash water with the white underwear, I threw my black sweatshirt into the laundry with some white fabric. When it was done, the piece sparkled a flawless, glistening white.

Then I thought, "Every time I make a quilt, no matter how carefully I prepare my fabrics, I always have some sort of dye disaster." So I dug through my fabrics looking for dark ones, greens and blues and purples, that had not yet been prewashed and might be prone to bleeding. I put them into a

- - - -

pot on the stove and boiled them. I boiled them some more. The water glistened colorless and sweet.

"I will just have to be really radical about this," I thought, and I threw a collection of solid black fabrics into the water. They boiled and boiled. The water simmered, clear as a mountain stream.

I was nearing the end of my resources. I called upon my husband, Bill, who fancies himself to be a mad scientist. He loves to experiment, so he took over the project. He boiled a pair of dingy, old black socks. Though he sterilized the socks perfectly, the water remained crystalline.

Next, he rooted in the bins in the back of the downstairs closet where I keep old art orphans (hairless paint brushes, dirty erasers, and scraps of construction paper). The black construction paper went into the cookpot. He boiled, and he stirred like the witches in Macbeth stirred their "eye of newt and toe of frog." He steamed and he boiled. The water turned color at last. It was a rich, deep red.

Onions skins turned the water golden; tea turned it a glowing, warm-brown.

Bill mixed and matched his brews standing over his steaming pot, stirring fabric in soggy swirls, tea and onion skins and construction paper and soggy socks. I put on my nightie. The hour was growing late. Undaunted, Bill still steamed and stirred.

He brewed up a batch of coffee grounds and added a touch of the red water from the craft paper. Dipping quickly and drying, dipping and drying, he at last produced a pale shade of the perfect tattle-tale gray we needed. I went to bed. He steamed and stirred more fabric.

When I woke the next morning, he presented me with a gift. It was a length of dirty-gray fabric, which I am now cutting into little pieces. I will match the little pieces to my border-print pieces and sew them all back together again. No one will ever dream of the cleverness that produced exactly the right shade of dishwater gray, and they will miss the best pleasure of all, seeing Bill standing in the kitchen at the witching hour, double, doubling, toiling and troubling, watching his cauldron boil and bubbling. To the viewer, it will simply look like a perfect, gray-brown mushroom color, a successful match of exactly the right colors. To me, it will be magic.

Time and Tide

If you have had a man in your life with a smooth, shaven face, you may have wondered what it feels like to kiss a man with a beard. I just found out!

Friends invited Bill and me to spend ten days with them on their boat. Since electricity was limited to battery power, Bill announced that he thought it would be expedient if he conserved that power and, instead of plugging in his razor every morning, he would grow a beard. I think he has always had a secret yearning to grow a beard, and he must have imagined that, with it, he would look like King Arthur or a dashing movie pirate. He knew exactly what sort of style he wanted.

For ten days, he groomed, occasionally using his disposable razor to trim around the edges. He lengthened his sideburns, and his new beard encircled and covered his chin. By the end of those ten days, Bill looked like a derelict sitting on a bench outside the liquor store. His beard had turned into a salt-and-pepper colored, porcupine kind of thing. Instead of flowing soft and silky, it bristled like a medieval war machine, and I can tell you right now, I felt as if I were kissing a scouring pad. Some men are handsome in beards. Bill is not.

I suppose that ten days is not really a fair test of a beard. I am sure that a debonair man sporting a more glorious facial decoration would argue that a good beard takes time. He would say that a true masterpiece requires careful, thoughtful planning, meticulous care and patience, and I am sure he would be right.

- - - -

As quilters, you and I already know this. We can whip out a quilt-in-a-day, spinning the design out of the computer, cutting it out with a rotary cutter, and stitching it together with fast, fiery stitches on the machine. That quick quilt will be soft and bright and warm, but our true quilt masterpieces take thoughtful planning and meticulous care. No matter how much we try to hurry the process, no matter what short-cuts and clever tools we use, those minutes must still add up to an investment of dedicated time. We have to be patient for the really good things in life to happen.

When I make a quilt, it will take at least twice the number of hours that I have set aside for it. I know that I tend to be overly optimistic about how much I can accomplish, and I make up for my poor planning by working late into the night. In the blush of anticipation, in the excitement of holding this wonderful, finished quilt in my hands, I forget the time element.

Bill has shaved off his beard, thank goodness. For him, wearing a beard was a whim, and it was not worth the effort. Making a quilt, on the other hand, is worth every second of its planning and stitching. As much as we would like to believe in marvels, we are not going to win the Time Lottery. We are not going to suddenly fall heir to a windfall of miraculous moments. Time to make a quilt adds up to minutes and days and weeks. When we quilt, time flows around us and through our fingers. Quilting time is precious time.

Oh, Chute

One thing that has pleased me about our house since we first moved into it forty years ago is the laundry chute. The first morning in the house, I scooped up assorted dirty clothing, opened the small door in the wall, and tossed in the laundry. It was very satisfying. Later that morning, I went down two stories into the basement to wash clothes. The basket on the floor beneath the chute was empty.

I went back upstairs and pushed my head into the little cubbyhole door. It was like peering into one of those ancient torture devices that looks like a mummy case lined with iron spikes. The chute was made from aluminum tubing shoved between the wall studs from the bedroom opening to the basement, hammered into place by driving nails willy-nilly through the metal channel.

For a while, I used a long, flexible strip of metal to poke and poke until the laundry dislodged and fell through, As time wore on, I discarded the improvised ramrod and simply collected the laundry, carried it down to the kitchen, and threw it down the basement stairs. Then the laundry chute became a wonderful source of communication.

We have, in the basement, an enormous, pine-paneled room where all of our daughters and a variety of foreign students have slept, dormitory-style. It is a very nice room, but communication with anyone downstairs was difficult. One day we realized that we could simply open the laundry chute

door and holler, "Telephone for you!" or "Bathroom's free."
We had become creative problem solvers.

Creative problem solving is something every quilter learns.
Sometimes I think I quilt because I love the challenge of
figuring out how to do things. For example, I was showing
friends an antique Lotus Flower quilt one evening. When the
lamplight picked up the shadows of the quilting, I realized
that the quilting design was drawn from the quilt maker's set
of china dishes. She was my kind of woman, relying on her
imagination, the kind of quilter who used her pot lids to
draw circles.

Our quilt stores display all kinds of gadgets. Rotary cutters
make preparation faster and more precise than scissors. Little
plastic things with toothed rollers leave chalk lines on our
fabrics, and magnetic pincushions attract and subdue spilled
pins. While grateful for these clever, bubble-packaged tools,
no commercial device gives me quite the satisfaction that I
get when I invent my own method to deal with my quilts.
Though the coated threads that we have nowadays are nearly
tangle-free I have accumulated a drawer full of candle stubs
for waxing my thread. My sewing drawer harbors pliers to
pull needles and a little cutting tool for clipping patterns out
of magazines. It holds tweezers for plucking at odd threads, a
magnifying glass, an emery board, a collar stay, a hole punch,
a popsicle stick, and a discarded mascara brush. All of these
have been solutions to some of my quilting problems.

Quilters must be inventors, and every time you and I plan

out the piecing schemes for quilt blocks, or figure out how to heal our sore fingers, or how to remove stubborn pencil marks, we are inventing. We are problem solving. We are coping.

Today's magazines are filled with articles about staying physically fit and healthy. We hear the same old incantation, "Use it or lose it." There are full-color pictures and diagrams that illustrate how to touch our toes, bend our knees, do sit-ups, and stretch. We are admonished to jog each morning or to practice the disciplined, fluid movements of Tai Chi. These rituals are supposed to keep our bodies strong and vibrant. I will admit that my body is not particularly strong or vibrant, but my mind does daily knee bends and deep stretches. I exercise my mind with problem solving.

Our useless laundry chute has become a valuable holler-downer. Much of my everyday litter has become tools for creative uses. I tug at needles, tack fabric together, and stitch patchwork pieces into patterns with the ordinary things around me. You and I—those of us who figure out how to sew hundreds of fabric scraps together and then wrestle that multipieced, unruly top into a manageable, beautiful quilt—are grapplers. We are discoverers. We are explorers and scientists. Our quilts are born in our hearts, and they are conjured up in our minds. Imagine that!

Leftovers

The end of the year is a time for leftovers. The winter holidays seem like one long foodfest beginning with Thanksgiving and progressing through the month of December all the way to the celebration of welcoming-in of the new year. It is a time of overeating and self-indulgence. When each feast is over, we stash half-filled casserole dishes and little packages of goodies in the refrigerator so that we can snack on the turkey scraps and leftover tidbits on subsequent evenings.

Last year, we ate the Thanksgiving meal at a friend's house, and we came home carrying cottage cheese cartons and foil packets filled with enough good food to provide a second scrumptious meal on Friday night. I was busy all day Friday quilting on my Christmas quilt, but at five o'clock, I peered inside the refrigerator. I was planning to do a fast microwave reheat of leftovers. I wanted to enjoy them, all hot and fragrant, and then settle in for the evening to do another hour or so of quilting.

I shuffled through the dishes on the refrigerator shelves. "I can't find the beans," I said to Bill. "Oh?" he said. "And what's happened to the pearl onions?" I'd stored some lovely creamed onions in their melty butter sauce, but there, in the bottom of the dish, lay one solitary onion looking back at me.

"I'm sorry" said Bill. "After you went to sleep last night, I got up and ate them. Everything was so good, I couldn't help myself. You'd better check the yams while you're at it, and see if there's enough left for dinner."

This is the time of day when I get hungry and grouchy. My ultimate fantasy of living where a maid would summon me nightly to a lovely, fully-prepared dinner has never materialized, so for me, the next best thing is to open my refrigerator door and find completely ready leftovers for my dinner, ready to heat at the touch of the microwave button. This night, there were no leftovers . . . at least not enough for a meal.

This is the season for leftovers, not only leftover food, but leftover fabric, too. Somehow as I approach the holidays each year, I find myself finishing a big quilt project. I begin one each year in the autumn when the sun drifts lower in the sky and the wind blows and the leaves fall. I begin the project because I need solace knowing that I will soon be dealing with the darkness of winter. All October and November I work feverishly on my quilt, hoping to get it quilted and out of the frame before the seasonal activities begin. I need the quilt frame space for family fun, and I need space in my mind for my own peace and the satisfaction of accomplishment.

Fabric leftovers are mysterious things. Unlike food leftovers, they don't seem to go away. To clear some of the lint from my mind, I have a routine that I follow when I finish a quilt. I put away my sewing tools and vacuum the debris from the floor. Then I fold all the fabric scraps of reasonable size and sort them into color piles. These I pack into my cupboards, cramming them into the gaps and holes in the stacks of materials that are already there. Once, those stacks were neat and even, with their edges straight, easily viewed, and readily accessible. Now they are jumbled, and when I open the door, I can trigger an avalanche. Closing that cupboard door and having it stay shut requires determination, manipulation, and sometimes just plain brute force.

Sometimes I make my quilt out of fabric that I purchased especially for that project. When the quilt is done, I fold what's left and it, too, goes in my cupboard. Sometimes, I dig into those ragamuffin piles, sift through them, and play with these choices for a scrap quilt. When my quilt is done, the remnants get folded, also, and stashed. It seems no matter how carefully I plan, no matter how meticulously I use my fabrics, at the end of a project, there is always more leftover fabric than I had before I started. My stash is out of control.

My thesis is that no matter how much leftover food one has, with a little bit of nibbling, it will eventually disappear, and the refrigerator will be empty. However, leftover fabric never goes away. It multiplies. It grows and swells to fill all available space. The good news is that you, your children, and your children's children will never run out of quilting material. Fabric is forever.

Chapter 6

FOR THE LOVE OF QUILTING

10 Things to Do with a Blizzard

WEATHER REPORT: Temperature is falling. Strong winds gusting up to 45 miles per hour. Blowing snow. Visibility zero. Snow emergency declared. Motorists are warned to stay off the road.

What's a quilter to do. . . .

1. Leaf through those old quilt magazines. Dream a little. Imagine the warmth, the comfort of having that lovely quilt you've carried in your head.

2. Call a friend to tell her about it, and while you're on the phone, remember that you are hungry.

3. Have a hot cup of something: coffee, tea, cocoa. Eat something fattening. Listen to the wind in the chimney and marvel at the white sky. Remember that you should be doing something useful. So,

4. Sew a button back on a shirt and

5. While you're at your sewing, look at all of your projects in progress. Sort out the one that cries out loudest to you. Decide to get moving on it. First step is . . .

6. Get out your thread. Look at those tangly, dangling ends. Carefully rewrap the thread ends around those soft plastic spools with the broken notches.

7. Clean out the lint that is packed into the teeth of your sewing machine. Oil your machine. You'll feel so good about it, that you'll put another drop of oil into each of the little

holes. The oil will run down the needle and the machine will smell funny, but it will sound sweet as a symphony when it runs. While you're being wonderfully neat . . .

8. Pull all of those pieces of fabric off your closet shelves. Press and fold them neatly. Clip off the loose threads and jagged ends. File them in color-coordinated piles. Put them perfectly in place on your shelf. Vacuum the room. Now,

9. Stand back and admire. Your threads, your fabric, your machine and tools, your magazines are in place. Your workspace looks like *House Beautiful*. Isn't it exciting? Isn't it inspiring? Your creative juices will begin to boil and . . .

10. You will get out your patterns, your thread, your scissors. You will spread fabric across the table and the chairs and the floor. Oh, it will be wonderful. Right then and there you will begin another project.

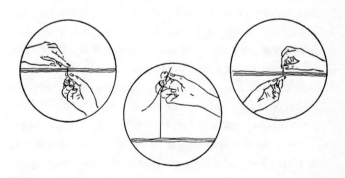

The Unkindest Cut of All

Have you ever thought how really personal your scissors are? You say, "Don't use my Kleenex, and don't use my comb—and, most of all, don't touch my scissors!" Your very own scissors feel right. You've worked them free so that they no longer bind up with newness. Maybe you've dropped a spot of oil in the joint and chopped them open and shut. Perhaps you have figured out just where the burr is on the blade, the burr you keep forgetting to get sharpened away. You've used them and you've used them, and they feel good.

I have a big collection of scissors. I can't recall where they all came from. There's the pair that had a rusty blade. I used an SOS pad to shine it. Don't ever shine your scissors with an SOS pad! Another pair developed a crooked snout when it dropped off the table and landed in the floor like a spear. There's a pair with a broken tip that I used as a screwdriver on my sewing machine. There's a wonderful pair I rescued from total disrepair, and when they were sharpened, they were like a surgical instrument. Some of my scissors are orphans that just appeared on my doorstep. Some are old friends.

Of course, I have my favorite scissors, too. They are a pair I cannot possibly sew without. I panic if I mislay them. They move open and shut smoothly, and they are wondrously sharp. They fit my hands. I use them for everything. I carry them with me everywhere, and when I work, I spread my fabric smoothly for them. I lay my work out in orderly fashion. I work with my scissors patiently and in good light. I treat them kindly, and I put them away in their sheath. I am gentle with them.

And last week they repaid me. I spread my work before me on my ironing board. I lined up my fabric just so, marked clearly. I clipped away so carefully. And—I cut my ironing-board cover right in half!

IQ Test

I am a very eager person. Excitability must be my primary gene. There is so much in life to be curious about, to find pleasure in, and to be surprised by, that moments of each day are filled to the brim with promise.

A couple of weeks ago, I was leaning off the bow of a ferryboat watching the water froth and swirl. One of the ferrymen insisted that I stand back properly behind the guard chain. When I threatened to creep back after he went away to the engine room or in the wheelhouse or whatever, he said, "There's a good deal of the kid in you, isn't there?"

He's probably right if he meant that I love discovering what the next moment is going to hold, and the next moment, and the next. How about you? Do you find new things wonderful? Can you hardly stand to wait for a holiday? Or a birthday? It's not just the gifts you may be getting, but the ones you are giving. It's lovely to see the surprise and delight on the face of a person you planned and shopped for.

Oh, the anticipation when you order something lovely from a catalog! Do you rush to the door when you hear the mailman at your box?

Of course, you do! You are a quilter. Excitement is part of your creative, joyful self. When I told a friend that I sometimes cut a hole in a quilt, she asked me why I would want to do that. I was astonished. (She was not a quilter.) I explained to her that I don't do it on purpose. I am just so excited and impatient when I am finished with the quilting that I accidentally stab the quilt when I am taking it out of the frame. Obviously impatience has its pleasures and its challenges. Anyway, here is a test to measure your own IQ (Impatience Quotient). My score is pretty high. Let's see how you do.

1. If you get a wonderful idea at two in the morning, can you turn over and go to sleep, knowing that the idea will still be there in the morning, or do you get up right then to write it down and try it out?

2. Do you drive all the way across town to the other quilt shop because the closer one doesn't have your special fabric and you need it right now?

3. When you come in the door with a bag full of fabric for your next project, can you wait several hours to wash and iron your material, or do you hang your coat over the back of the chair, move aside the dishes on the table, and start to cut out your quilt immediately?

4. Do you delay sending out your favorite scissors to be sharpened because you simply cannot sew without them, and you can't bear the thought of putting off your quilting/piecing/appliquéing?

5. If you drop your needle on the floor, do you take time to get down on your knees and hunt carefully, or do you simply pull another needle out of the pack and warn the family to wear shoes?

6. When dinner is over, do you stack the dishes in the sink and go quilt, because you know the dishes won't be any dirtier in the morning than they are right at that moment?

7. Do you get so excited when you are finally ready to border your pieced blocks that sometimes you cut out a border strip ½″ too narrow? or too short?

8. Can you wait to pull your basting threads out until your quilt is finished, or do you pull them out as you work?

9. If you put the last quilting stitch in your quilt at midnight, can you wait until tomorrow to take it out of the frame?

10. Do you rush out to show people your quilt the moment you have finally bound and signed it?

If your answers tell you that, like me, you are an impatient person, you already know that you have had to develop certain talents for coping: creative piecing, remedial appliqué, and flexibility. If you are an impatient person who bounds with enthusiasm, who leaps without looking, strange as it may seem, there is a bonus. It comes with the challenge of dealing with insufficient border fabric or handling bleeding fabric when you remove your pencil lines too hastily or devising a new design because the old one is buried somewhere under the new fabrics piled on the corner of your table. Then, in the creative moment that you deal with the challenge, something new and exciting happens: Right out of your brain comes an idea of your very own and it works. Ah, impatience and the joy of creative coping . . . there's the blessing.

Drawn and Quartered

Have you noticed lately that almost every time we pick up a new publication we can find an analytical article that divides humanity into four parts? We have been divided into four color seasons, for instance. I am a Spring coloring, a Vibrant Spring with a touch of Autumn. Another book indicates that I am a Clear-Bright as opposed to a Muted.

A funny book I sent to my sister classified people as seasonings. In it I discovered that I am a Parsley with a touch of Garlic.

If we were flowers, I most certainly would be a Talisman Rose rather than a Gardenia or Holly Berry. As for animals, I am not a Lion or a Timid Rabbit; rather, I am a Pushover Pussy Cat.

The morning paper has put a new wrinkle on the face of humanity or maybe on the brain of humanity. It has a chart by which we divide ourselves into the four portions of the brain. Sounds very scientific, doesn't it?

Well, I, for one, am a quilter, and rather than speak the language of the gourmet, the botanist, the zoologist, or the pathologist, let's talk quilters' talk about our personalities, our compulsions, our pleasures. Surely we can divide us up into quarters, and once analyzed, we will be able to tell whom we should show our next quilt to and whom we should never sit beside at a quilt frame. Answer the following questions as honestly as you can, writing down the answers so that you can add up your responses to determine your personal Quilt Category.

- - - -

1. Your favorite pieced design is:
   a. anything that has 120 small pieces
   b. Double Wedding Ring
   c. Amish Bars
   d. Log Cabin
2. Your favorite appliqué design is:
   a. wild geometrics
   b. Sunbonnet Sue
   c. *broderie perse*
   d. landscapes
3. You prefer to work with:
   a. home-dyed colors
   b. scrap-quilt fabrics
   c. crisp, glossy solids
   d. a spectrum of sherbet colors
4. Your favorite shade of blue is:
   a. navy
   b. varieties of blue
   c. peacock blue
   d. powder blue
5. You think computers are good for:
   a. innovative quilt design
   b. simplifying repetitive block layouts
   c. balancing your checkbook
   d. other people

6. Your favorite quilting design is:
   a. creative interpretation
   b. Feathered Wreath
   c. contrasting motion to pieced designs
   d. outline quilting
7. You prefer to quilt:
   a. unconventionally
   b. with eighteen stitches to the inch
   c. in bright, contrasting threads
   d. doesn't matter so long as it holds the quilt together neatly
8. Your favorite time to do the dishes is:
   a. never; use paper plates
   b. immediately
   c. tomorrow
   d. hide them in the oven until you get around to them
9. Your favorite time to quilt is:
   a. all the time
   b. all the time
   c. all the time
   d. all the time

To score: Total up your answers under a, b, c, and d. The majority of your points will indicate your personal Quilt Category.

A. *UNBLEACHED MUSLIN*: You are Spartan in your approach to design, straightforward in dealing with life as well as with quilts, skillful in balancing colors, relationships, and time. An Unbleached Muslin is a person who is definitely well-ordered and purposeful.

B. *CALICO*: This person is traditional and meticulous. She enjoys a challenge and finds that an investment of time and effort in her work is worth every moment and ounce of energy she devotes to it. Calico loves to blend a variety of patterns and people into a cheerful world of complementary colors.

C. *POLISHED COTTON*: This quilter is a sophisticate. She handles colors with a deft eye and purchases her fabric without wincing at cost. For generations, Polished Cottons have created stunning quilts with flair. Polished Cottons have confidence.

D. *DOUBLE KNITS*: This is a comfortable person. This person uses up scraps of fabric and meal leftovers with equal aplomb, producing happy sorts of creations. Double knits like the world, the state of the nation, their homes, friends, and their quilts. Double knits are definitely pleasant people.

Out of these four categories of quilters, one of my best friends is an Unbleached Muslin. Last week, I met a Double Knit who not only makes charming quilts, she also makes the best pot of coffee that ever bubbled on a stove. I, myself, tend to be a Calico with overtones of Polished Cotton and a dash of Double Knits. Whatever we discover about ourselves, we must remember that we are all human (at least after we have had our breakfasts). We each thread our needles by passing a tiny thread through a small hole in its end, no matter how difficult it sometimes is. Each of us prefers to quilt, rather than eat, most of the time.

As quilters, we are part of the larger Fabric of Life. As Unbleached and Polished, Calico and Double Knits, we belong to the larger category of Good Cloth. Among the world-class materials, we are the privileged. In answering this quiz we have identified our own special styles and preferences, but we are still bound together by the fact that every one of us likes to save, fold, pat, cut, piece, stitch, and cherish our quilts. Because each of us is fashioned from the Good Cloth category, we can admire each other's quilts, experiment, and explore. Ours is the Good Cloth Life.

Creature Comforts

We've had a long line of cats in our family—that is, not "long line" in the way of lineage, but rather in the way of time. They have marched nose to heel through our house across the years.

There was St. David, a soft gray pussy. He was a gentle, sweet sort of cat that looked rather like the picture on the box of Tender Vittles. David sought affection. He was very persistent about it. He crawled through open windows at night and snuggled up to our slumbering neighbors. David was not popular.

Cleopatra was sleek and black. Her lithe body rippled beneath her glossy fur. She was aloof and not particularly friendly. She spent her days in the backs of closets and beneath beds. She was more of a ghost-guest than an active family member, and since she preferred her privacy, we came to accept it.

Henry Ford was orange. His chief attribute was his deep-chested motor that resonated through his whole body. You could hear him all the way in the next room. My kitchen became an obstacle course on Sunday mornings as I tried to fix breakfast. He wound around my legs, rubbing and rolling and droning.

But Thomas Edison was a joy. Thomas was huge and golden, and he had a ringed tail of long, glistening fur. He was a charmer. He loved you with such passion, such devotion, that you could not turn him away. When guests sat in our living room, Thomas would hurtle himself into their laps, plaster himself against their chests, and, nose to nose, he would rumble deeply and delightedly. After the initial shock, even the non-cat lovers among our friends were won over. Thomas's charm could not be denied.

The point of all this is that as different as they were, they shared a common fancy. All these cats loved quilts. They loved them from the first tiny scrap to the soft elegance when the quilt was spread out fully on my bed. Consider the piecing of a quilt. Remember the piles of neatly stacked pieces, carefully cut and counted? Cats love pieces. They love to roll in them, paws throwing them high into the air. See them flutter! The missing triangle can be found behind the wastebasket, pawed and chewed into a soggy scrap. Have you tried to iron a chewed, soggy scrap back into piecing shape?

A spool of thread is an adventure for a cat. A spool of thread left untended in an empty house arouses feline ecstasy. Do you realize how long 425 yards of thread is? Do you realize how many times 425 yards of thread can be batted around the table legs, behind chairs, under the couch, and back again? In the interest of a tranquil mind, thriftiness must be abandoned. Rewinding 425 yards of thread onto an empty spool is an impossible task. I know. I've tried it.

Cats love pincushions, too. If you are a pussy psychologist, perhaps you can explain to me why a cat will straddle a pincushion and meticulously extract all of the pins, one at a time, with his teeth. One of our cats was so dedicated to emptying pincushions that I saw him actually attacking our long-needled cactus in the living-room window.

But most of all cats love quilts in the quilt frames. It took quite a while for my cats to train me to accept this. I spent some years determined to keep contented cats from curling into the comforts of my quilts-in-progress. As soon as my back was turned (and sometimes they brazenly did it before my very eyes), they leapt gracefully into the center of my frame, circled several times, settled in, and rumbled deeply. I am not fond of paw prints. I take a dim view of cat hairs on my quilts. I devised ingenious deterrents. I stacked cans, all sorts—peaches, spinach, creamed corn—across the top of the quilt as a sort of battleground. The cats curled into the nooks and crannies they assumed I had created especially for them. When I went to bed at night, I propped one end of the frame high up on a cardboard box. It made a sort of children's slippy-slide. The cats were tenacious. They clung and clawed. I took to keeping a pile of things to throw. There were rolled socks, spoons, empty spools, and shoes. One day I threw a book and caught a cat between the shoulder blades. I was horrified that I had been so impulsive as to throw a precious book. The cat picked himself up off the floor, eyed me with disdain, and flung himself back into the middle of the frame.

We eventually came to terms, of course, the cats and I. I gave in. They taught me to turn back the covering sheet on the quilt just far enough to allow me to quilt on one block. The cats lay on the quilt at my elbow. They smiled. They snuggled. They watched with one open eye. They purred deliciously. Cats have good taste. They love quilts.

You Are Cordially Invited
to a Fashion Show

When I answered the doorbell, the woman standing on my front step said, "How nice! You look so comfortable in your jogging suit."

"I never jog," I said. "This is a quilting suit."

Then, standing right there in my front doorway, I had a vision. In it there was a woman in a pearl necklace and a flowered hat. She was standing at a podium, and there was a spotlight on her as she was narrating a fashion show.

"And here is Helen," she was saying. "Tonight, she is wearing a lavender quilting suit and it is complemented with charming accessories. Helen is wearing her thimble and her chatelaine and she is carrying her scissors and her Basic Sewing Kit.

"And for warm weather wear, we have Helen in her Q-shirt. It has short sleeves and is made of lightweight knit that allows her freedom of movement around the quilt frame. Many women who wear this shirt refer to it by its other name, the T-shirt. Not so for Helen! She wears her Q-shirt with a pair of comfortable shorts. The accessory for this casual outfit is a soft, fleecy towel, attractive and so convenient for placing beneath the legs on a hot day to prevent sudden pain when standing up from a sticky plastic kitchen chair beside the quilt frame.

"For more formal wear, Helen wears a long gown. Although we ordinarily think of long gowns for night wear, this outfit is high-fashion for early morning. When a quilter wakes early and slips down to quilt before the sun is high, she may find herself working well into the day in this attractive long gown. If you find that this outfit is somewhat less than acceptable for greeting the meter reader or the delivery man, the clever little watch that Helen is wearing will make you a better clock-watcher.

"For fabric shopping, this next outfit is ideal. When worn with a little blouse, this wraparound skirt is warm for winter and cool for summer. It allows freedom of movement for wrestling with bolts of fabric and carrying large paper sacks. Accessorizing this outfit is a charming set of car keys and a full wallet.

"For preparing a quilt. Helen wears a simple, very basic outfit that allows her to creep across the floor on her knees, patting her three layers neatly and smoothly and basting her quilt with long spider-web patterns. This little garment is known as a slip, and it is trimmed with lace in a delicate butterfly pattern.

"And now, finally, today's *pièce de résistance*! Helen is wearing her 'Let's show off the quilt' dress. It is simple but elegant with unadorned lines and gentle colors. The sweet softness of this dress forms an uncluttered background for the ultimate accessory, The New Quilt. This outfit will go anywhere, any time and any place, and it will highlight the perfectly shaded colors, the tiny stitches, the sharp points and the clever design of the quilt. The headwear for this ensemble is, of course, a halo."

Yield Not to Temptation

I bought myself a new sewing machine recently. As machines go, this one is a "stretch-limo." Let me take you back to the beginning of my life-with-the-mechanical-needle. Years ago, farther back than I like to acknowledge, I marched into a sewing-machine store. I was about to be married, and I knew that I had better be able to provide clothing and apartment decorating touches economically. That day, I bought myself a little Featherweight machine. It was one of the best moves of my life. Would you believe that in some forty years the machine has never had to be repaired?

Some years later, but still a long, long time ago, new machines were marketed that not only sewed in straight lines, but had a needle that swung back and forth to make a zigzag edge. I marched myself into a sewing-machine store again. This one had a big plate-glass window, and ladies sat at sewing machines doing wondrous things with them. There was a big sale that day, and the trade-in offer on my Featherweight was something like $5 and it didn't make sense to practically give it away. Still, I couldn't justify having *two* machines if I bought something expensive. A big splurge would have netted me a machine that stitched fancy embroidery stitches when little metal cams were inserted somewhere into the machine's interior. For less than $100, however, I felt that I could afford a simple machine with a swing needle.

It was thrilling to lug home the new "monster." It sat on my kitchen table all big and heavy and white and impressively modern. It sewed a straight stitch fairly competently.

- - - -

The zigzag stitch was somewhat less successful, but in spite of the hard puckery edge it created, at least this was something my first machine couldn't do. Actually, I learned to use the zigzag stitch to darn holes in my children's jeans, which, I suppose, actually paid for the machine over the years.

I became quite comfortable with the white zigzag "clunker." I learned a certain amount of maintenance using only an oilcan, a toothbrush for lint removal, and a screwdriver. I bought a wonderful little book that explained what happens to bobbins and feed dogs, and the machine and I came to understand each other. I think it even came to respect me as I grew adept at changing its belt, although it became covered with black rubber grime from used-up, disintegrated belts. And, it became dotted with my grungy fingerprints.

Occasionally, I would have to haul the "thing" into the repairman. Usually, it was because I had jammed a pin into the feed dogs and nicked the inside, or some other dumb thing that even the most neophyte sewer knows better than to do. Each time that I hauled that machine in, the repairman would say, "Why did you buy this piece of junk?" and each time I nipped back with my standard reply, "Because you sold it to me."

Not so long ago, as I was sitting and sewing, I stepped on the foot pedal of the white monster, and it hesitated. When I examined the pedal I decided that it needed a little oil, nothing big. Still, there were other signs of aging: scratches, wiggly parts, and a definite tendency to get hot if I sewed furiously, at top speed, for any length of time.

I could probably have gone on playing nursemaid to that

machine, and it may have sewn things adequately for another decade; maybe I was looking for an excuse. Anyway, I went out that day and shopped for another one. I ordered the fanciest, most gorgeous machine I could find. When I came home, I had a brief moment of, well, not repentance, but of sheer horror over the financial commitment that I had made.

I justified my expenditure: I reminded myself that this is now, and that money is more expensive now. I noted that with things becoming more costly every day, if I waited until the old white creature expired, a new one would be even more expensive than it is now. It was obvious, too, that for anyone who spends hours every day at the sewing machine as I do, life will be easier, faster, neater, and better. It was extremely easy to soothe my guilty conscience.

The new stretch-limo has been delivered (and the old tin lizzie has been given away to a daughter who has an affection for it and figures that having it for a few months before its demise will be pleasant). The limo is set up in my back room, sparkling clean. It winks its red light at me. It came with fourteen pieces of literature, a pile of pamphlets, and four books. There are five videos, too.

There are ten fancy presser feet in the accompanying plastic toolbox. I go into a cold sweat when I look at them. It will take a lifetime to learn to deal with all of this incredible technology. I thought, when I began, that all I wanted to do was make my quilting projects simpler and more accurate. Force of habit makes me slow the wheel with my hand and jiggle the foot pedal. Actually the wheel speed is flawless and the spiffy foot pedal does everything exactly right.

– – – –

It is an awesome thing to have a sewing machine that is smarter than I am. It is also more beautiful. Its whirrr is a siren's song. It calls to me, lures me. I should be content to piece perfect blocks or to machine quilt the grandchildren's Christmas quilts so that they will be strong enough to toss into the washing machine. As they wear, I will not have invested the blood, sweat, and tears of hand-quilted comfort. As the machine sings and winks, the tucking and overlocking and ruffling and embroidering devices are tempting me. I had once convinced myself that I could buy clothing for my family cheaper than I could make it, but I no longer believe that. The family is so comfortable in this aging home that no decorating seems necessary. If something is worn, surely I can throw a quilt over it, hang a quilt in front of it, or sew a quilt patch into it. Still my clever Beauty sits there in my workroom, humming to me, preening, lifting its skirts a bit to show me its shapely attachments.

What I really need to do, I think, is to get down to business on a new quilt. I need to work hard on it, let it occupy my mind during all waking hours, become obsessed with it, and then, maybe, just maybe I can resist the temptation to ruffle and pleat and gather. Perhaps instead I can find new ways, wonderful ways, to piece and set and bind. Perhaps I can invent new ways to make my points sharp and accurate, to make my quilts even up the sides, my corners straight and square. With the help of all this precision, this mechanical brilliance, maybe now, at last, I will be able to fit forty-eight hours' worth of glorious quiltmaking into my daily twenty-four.

For the Mature Audience

Thrift, hence saving, is a virtue. Sometimes a virtue is questionable.

For instance, I look into my fabric cupboard. There, I can see that my saving, virtuous as it may be, is out of control, and I can tell you here and now that it takes a mature person to amass that much fabric. It did not happen overnight. Bit by bit, over forty-five years I have saved it up—though the double knits, the polyesters, and the super-heavy drapery fabrics have been assigned to boxes in the basement, perhaps never to see the light of day again.

Here, on my fabric shelves are bits of old skirts in lovely shades of red, garish green prints in 36″-wide widths from the 1970s, scraps of hard percale sheets that had just the right print but were tough to quilt through. There are new fabrics, too, the ones I found last week at the quilt store and couldn't resist, the wonderful mottled boggy-brown print blouse from the Goodwill store, the great feed sacks that another quilter wanted out of her fabric shelves and gifted to me. There are fabrics with "things" on them like light bulbs and sheep and ice cream cones.

Someday I may need a light bulb or a sheep or an ice cream cone. Whatever am I going to do, though, with the Statue of Liberty print from 1986? It will probably not be appropriate again until 2086, and I doubt that I will be around then.

I guess that the redeeming factor in owning this splendiferous stash of fabric is that I really do use it. I keep it in large plastic storage bins piled on shelves in my closet from floor to ceiling. To reach the top bins, I stand on a short stepladder and wrestle them down. Almost always there is a disaster—I tip off the ladder, sprawl, and do strange things to my shins, hips, knees, arms, and so on. Or I drop the bin onto my ironing board (which is why I have had to glue my iron back together).

I always do these dramatic things with a great deal of noise, which has shortened my family's life expectancy considerably. The statistics all say that it is not healthy to live with stress. They live with a lot of stress. I live with a lot of fabric.

Recently I received a questionnaire from The Housing Authority. It was one of those anonymous forms that cover a number of pages, and my first inclination was to throw the thing into the wastebasket. The questions on the form had to do with "housing for artists." With all of the poor people wandering the streets, I don't know why they are concerned with housing for artists, unless artists are poor people, too.

Anyhow, the questionnaire asked, "If I could design my own workspace/living space, what would I choose?" It had questions about heavy-duty wiring, which I don't need, and as I read on, I decided they were aiming their questions at sculptors and painters and people who do a lot of whacking and running of loud equipment. As a quilter, I felt that I needed to be represented, too. So I answered their questions.

Think about it! If you could design your own workspace, what would you put into it if money were no object? I was allowed, in the wrap-up of the questions, to list my five most important considerations, and I chose (1) a large empty wall for designing, (2) a high ceiling to allow me to hang my quilts for photography, (3) good natural light, (4) plenty of uninterrupted floor space for basting, and (5) STORAGE SPACE.

I pictured an entire wall of shelving, hip-high, with my fabric bins lined up and accessible. I could see them all, with their lids thrown back and all of the colors flashing out at me, winking and waving. I could reach them easily without threat to life and limb. I could flirt with them, spreading them out at my feet, melding the hues together, and when I was done, I would simply fold them back into their easy bins without gasping, struggling, and teetering.

In this wonderland of a workspace, my vices would indeed be virtues. My fabric would no longer be a self-indulgent hoard of cloth in disarray. My fabric would be well-organized and socially acceptable. It would be transformed from Adult material to a "G" rating: Great, Good, and Generally Gratifying. Now I would have a good, workable place to store it, and I would feel like a truly virtuous woman.

Physical Fitness

I looked in the mirror today and thought, "I'm gorgeous! Oh, I'm absolutely gorgeous!" Let me explain.

I've been bemoaning the fact that my quilt hips have gotten wider and softer. It all has to do with the inactivity of spending hours at the quilt frame and my calorie consumption during the quilting breaks. Not only was I not looking good but the situation was getting worse.

My husband Bill spends spare moments pedaling on an exercycle. He has offered to lower the seat so that I can ride it too, but though it may be sacrilege to all of you dyed-in-the-wool cyclists, I hate riding a bike. When I was very young, I spent wonderful days pedaling my balloon-tired Columbia bike around the countryside with my best friend Suey, but when I reached the age that I wanted to take classes at the college nearby, I bought myself one of those skinny, multi-geared things and rode it daily. Shifting a bike is not like shifting a car. In a car, you sit cradled in a comfortable seat, armored and safe. On a bike, you straddle the machine trying to keep your balance in the middle of very near and very threatening traffic while trying to decipher all of the positions of that little gear lever. To top it off, when you are through, the tops of your legs ache.

My decision to do something about my hips was made last Sunday. I was sitting at the quilt frame stitching on my latest quilt, and Bill was reading me the ads from the newspaper.

There, in big, bold primary colors was an ad for a ski-glider. The local discount store had a special, and the contraption was so cheap they were practically paying people to take them home. At least it seemed that way to me, as I eased my hips a little further forward in the chair and bent over the frame to read the paper.

I love cross-country skiing. I'm not very good at it, but I manage to stand up, move ahead, and fall down only occasionally—except for this past winter when I swooped down an icy hill and my skis went in opposite directions. I did amazing things to my body. That has been part of my excuse for not exercising—that my ski-knee hasn't recovered adequately. Actually, it has, you understand. I have just been making excuses.

Well, I pushed my chair out from under that quilt frame and went out and got in the car and drove to the discount store. There I pulled an enormous box off a shelf and wrestled it to the checkout counter. Just the exercise of getting the ski-glider out of the store must have burned up some of those calories and diminished my poundage some. My mother used to tell me that ladies do not sweat, they do not perspire, they merely glow. I can tell you that I was no lady.

So here is my ski-glider right beside my quilt frame in the back room. I did not need one more thing in this room. I have to walk crab-like through it now. My glider directions say that I am supposed to ski on the thing thirty minutes at a time, which is insanity. Thirty minutes straight on that machine at my age would destroy me. Instead, I stop periodically and get up from the frame and ski five minutes at a time. It's wonderful. I feel slender, firm, young, rather like that gorgeous young thing wearing the French-cut leotards in the ski-glider commercial on TV. This new activity is going to make a new and beautiful me. I've been skiing/quilting only three days, and already I can see the difference. It may have something to do with the fact that I am not using my quilting breaks for donut munching. I am lean; I am lovely. Who would have thought that relating quilting to another activity could be the way to a more glamorous me?

Starting from Square One

My granddaughter asked, "Will you teach me to quilt?" This young woman has talented hands. Even as a small child, she would stitch intricate counted-thread pictures. She knits glorious sweaters, but never has she quilted.

She loves the story about my daughters and their quilting marathon. When they were young, the week after Christmas was always difficult. The excitement of the gift giving was past, the weather too bitter to play outside, and the four restless girls were caged together. That year, each girl's big present was a box filled with five-inch squares of every fabric in my stash, which was considerable, even then.

I challenged each girl to put her own special squares together and make a quilt top, and then we would have a celebration on New Year's Day where I would help them tie their tops into comforters. It was a quiet week. They sorted their colors, played with them, and finally stitched them. On January 1, all four made themselves comforters. Those "quilts" can still be found on the shelves of their closets today.

For her high school graduation present, Else asked for quilt squares like I had given her mother. I filled a box with hundreds of squares of fabric, and periodically over the years, she has taken those squares out, moved them, arranged them, and put them back in their box without sewing them. So when Else married, I gave her a Featherweight sewing machine, a rotary cutter and mat, and some basic quilting supplies. I assumed that she knew what to do with them. Clever enough to figure out the sewing machine on her own, she tried sewing the squares together. But she needed help.

"Else," I asked, "what did they teach you in school?"

"They don't teach sewing in school anymore," she said, "just fashion design."

That announcement took my breath. Sewing is a basic survival skill! Even if you never intend to make clothing, its important to know good fabric to know about fading, shrinking, grain line, and good workmanship. Else needed some practical experience.

Lesson I: We met at a mill-ends store so that she could learn how to tell the textile treasures from the trash. Else didn't know the difference between a sateen and a double-knit, between a fine cotton weave and a slippery cotton/polyester blend. We roamed the aisles, turning over heaps of flat-folds and fingering through the fabrics, feeling loose fibers and pasty fillers, looking at weaves and labels, learning about selvedge markings and brand names, searching for flaws and misprints, and, in general, playing with fabric.

Lesson II: Else arrived early. She had her Featherweight machine and her rotary cutter, and I had spread out a rainbow of fabric on the floor. She chose fabrics to make two Four Patches, one by hand, and one by machine Her intersections were perfect, but her blocks were made in two shades of lavender. They were gentle and sweet, but she needed to learn how to be adventurous. We needed to experiment with color.

Lesson III: We sorted and splashed about in fabrics, making piles of gentle hues, and exciting, clashing, vibrating shades and tints. We looked at paintings by old masters and photographs of the world around us, seeing how the world is made up of a zillion shades of green. She began to "see" color, and she got excited. I got excited.

Lesson IV: Else tells me that she is serious, now. On this day, she cut triangles to piece of lavender and yellow. Quick to learn, she is a little less timid. Her points came together perfectly, and she discovered some important, practical things such as the scary importance of rotary cutter safety. She learned that patchwork can be an everyday, any day, part of our kitchen-table life.

What a renewal for me! I remember the magic and the excitement of the first time I sewed four squares of fabric together. Having met so many sophisticated, experienced quilters, I had forgotten the sweet moments of the first discoveries, but Else has been reaching me. She has given me a gift. I have seen her excitement grow as she has discovered the amazing possibilities that lie in simple shapes and colors and the miracle that our fingers can produce by putting them together. In watching her, and in seeing her find such joy, I have rediscovered quilting.

- - - -

ABOUT THE AUTHOR

⊠ ⊠ ⊠

Helen Kelley is a quiltmaker, lecturer, author, and instructor based in Minneapolis, Minnesota. Since she bought her first sewing machine—a Singer Featherweight—in 1946, she has made over 115 quilts and wall hangings, many of which are of masterpiece quality and have been displayed at shows both nationally and internationally.

Widely respected by the quilting community, Helen was the first president of the Minnesota Quilter's Guild and has received an abundance of awards for her quilts. In 1999, at the International Quilt Festival in Houston, Texas, her "Renaissance Quilt" was chosen as one of the 100 Best American Quilts of the Twentieth Century.

Helen's "Loose Threads" articles have appeared monthly in *Quilter's Newsletter Magazine* for twenty years. Written in wry and pertinent language, the column has long been a favorite of readers. Her previous books include *Scarlet Ribbons: American Indian Technique for Today's Quilters*; *Dating Quilts: From 1600 to the Present*; and two self-published books of flower patterns. She was also featured in Oxmoor House's *Quilt with the Best*. In addition, Helen's by-line has appeared in a variety of quilting publications, and her prize-winning quilts have been the subject of numerous photo essays.